Landbird Monitoring Protocol for Channel Islands National Park – Version 2.0

Natural Resource Report NPS/MEDN/NRR—2011/480

Timothy J. Coonan

National Park Service
Channel Islands National Park
1901 Spinnaker Drive
Ventura, CA, 93001

Linda C. Dye

National Park Service
Channel Islands National Park
1901 Spinnaker Drive
Ventura, CA, 93001

Steven G. Fancy

National Park Service
Inventory and Monitoring Division
1201 Oak Ridge Drive, Suite 150
Fort Collins, CO, 80525

December 2011

U.S. Department of the Interior
National Park Service
Natural Resource Stewardship and Science
Fort Collins, Colorado

The National Park Service, Natural Resource Stewardship and Science directorate publishes a range of reports that address natural resource topics of interest and applicability to a broad audience in the National Park Service and others in natural resource management, including scientists, conservation and environmental constituencies, and the public.

The Natural Resource Report Series is used to disseminate high-priority, current natural resource management information with managerial application. The series targets a general, diverse audience, and may contain NPS policy considerations or address sensitive issues of management applicability.

All manuscripts in the series receive the appropriate level of peer review to ensure that the information is scientifically credible, technically accurate, appropriately written for the intended audience, and designed and published in a professional manner.

The material in this report received formal peer review by subject-matter experts who were not directly involved in the collection, analysis, or reporting of the data, and whose background and expertise put them on par technically and scientifically with the authors of the information.

Views, statements, findings, conclusions, recommendations, and data in this report do not necessarily reflect views and policies of the National Park Service, U.S. Department of the Interior. Mention of trade names or commercial products does not constitute endorsement or recommendation for use by the U.S. Government.

This report is available from the internet website for the Mediterranean Coast I&M Network at http://science.nature.nps.gov/im/units/medn, and from the NPS Integrated Resource Management Applications (IRMA) data system at https://irma.nps.gov/App/Reference/Profile/2181856.

Please cite this publication as:

Coonan, T. J., Dye, L. C., and S. G. Fancy. 2011. Landbird monitoring protocol for Channel Islands National Park – Version 2.0. Natural Resource Report NPS/MEDN/NRR—2011/480. National Park Service, Fort Collins, Colorado.

NPS 159/112106, December 2011

Contents

Contents (continued)

Figures

Table

Appendixes

Standard Operating Procedures (SOPs)

The following SOPs are attached at the end of this document and are numbered individually to facilitate using them independently and revising or updating them.

Executive Summary

Channel Islands National Park was the first park in the National Park System to design and implement a long-term ecological monitoring program to track changes in the condition of terrestrial and marine natural resources that the park is responsible for managing. Monitoring of landbirds began on several of the islands in the park in 1993, and since then, the sampling design, methodology, database, and data analysis and reporting procedures have been reviewed and improved and are now formalized in this protocol document. In April 2000, a formal technical review of the landbird monitoring program at Channel Islands National Park was undertaken by eight renowned experts in bird monitoring who recommended that the park add some new point count sites using distance sampling in addition to the line transect surveys that had previously been used. Because of funding and staffing constraints, the full transition to the new sampling design, which involved establishing the new sampling sites and conducting monitoring at both the old and new sites for at least three years, was not fully completed until 2008. This protocol was written in 2011 to document the landbird monitoring methods conducted since 1993 and to formalize the methods that are now used to monitor landbirds on the five islands in the park. A new database in MS Access has been developed to store and summarize the landbird data, and statistical and graphing routines using the statistical package R have been developed to streamline the process for analyzing data and generating reports.

This protocol outlines the rationale, sampling design, field methods, data management and analysis procedures, and reporting procedures for monitoring landbirds at Channel Islands National Park. This protocol narrative describes the landbird monitoring program in relatively broad terms, following the protocol standards developed by the National Park Service Inventory and Monitoring Program (Oakley et al. 2003). The details of the sampling design, field methodology, and procedures for managing, analyzing, and reporting the data are addressed in a set of stand-alone Standard Operating Procedures (SOPs) that accompany this document.

Acknowledgments

This protocol for monitoring landbirds at Channel Islands National Park is primarily a compilation of sections from landbird monitoring protocols developed by other networks in the National Park Service Inventory and Monitoring Program, as well as material from various reports produced by Channel Islands National Park staff. The NPS I&M Program promotes consistency among the 32 I&M networks and encourages networks to build upon peer-reviewed and tested protocols developed by others to allow sharing and comparing of data service-wide. We incorporated material from the I&M Program's "prototype bird monitoring protocol" for the Heartland Network developed by Peitz et al. (2004), as well as material from protocols developed for the Sonoran Desert Network (Powell et al. 2007), North Coast and Cascades Network (Siegel et al. 2007), Great Lakes Network (Gostomski et al. 2010), Klamath Network (Stephens et al. 2010), and Sierra Nevada Network (Siegel et al. 2010). We thank all of the authors and peer reviewers of those protocols for their contributions to this protocol.

In April 2000, a group of renowned bird monitoring experts participated in a technical review of the landbird monitoring program that had been conducted at Channel Islands National Park since 1993, and provided the park with a number of recommendations that have since been incorporated into the monitoring and that are now formalized in this protocol document. For their contributions towards improving the landbird monitoring efforts at the park and throughout the National Park System, we thank Drs. John Bart, David DeSante, Steven Fancy, Paul Geissler, Robert Kuntz, Kathryn McEachern, C. J. Ralph, John Sauer, and Rodney Siegel.

We thank the many people at Channel Islands National Park whose contributions have allowed the park to conduct annual landbird monitoring. We specifically thank Kate Faulkner for her relentless support of ecological monitoring, Mitchell Dennis, Kara Randall, Dan Harper, Andrea Lehotsky, Carolyn Greene, Jen Savage, Helen Fitting and Sarah Hansen for their fieldwork, and all of the island staff who provide field support. Our thanks also to Laurie Kurilla for her patience and talent in creating and modifying queries to provide the report information, Rocky Rudolph for his assistance with figures, and Ulysses Huerta for his ability to keep the information and communications equipment and software working. We thank Doretta Burgess and dispatch personnel for their unwavering support and kindness, and boat captains Diane Brooks, Dwight Willey and Keith Duran. Transportation chief Rhonda Brooks keeps the whole transportations system afloat. We appreciate the wonderful logistical support provided by island staff, particularly Randy Nelson, Mark Senning, Randy Bidwell, and Earl Whetsell; and by the administration personnel who keep the purchasing and payment process going to support us all. And last but not least, we appreciate the assistance of Paul Geissler and the helpful peer reviews by Rodney Siegel, David Peitz, and Tom Philippi who took the time to make this a better protocol.

1. Background and Objectives

Issue being Addressed and Rationale for Monitoring Landbirds

Channel Islands National Park was the first park in the National Park System to design and implement a long-term ecological monitoring program to track changes in the condition of terrestrial and marine natural resources that the park is responsible for managing (Davis and Halvorson 1988, Davis 1989). National Park Service (NPS) Management Policies (NPS 2006) state that "The Service will also strive to ensure that park resources and values are passed on to future generations in a condition that is as good as, or better than, the conditions that exist today". National park managers need reliable scientific data and information on the status and trends in the condition of key park resources to address the overall management objective to maintain or improve the condition of natural and cultural resources, as a basis for conservation planning, and to inform stakeholders and the general public about the park's efforts and successes in meeting management objectives. Data collected in a consistent way over long time periods are fundamental to conservation and management because they provide the context for interpreting observed changes, and may provide the basis for initiating new management practices or changing existing practices (Carpenter 1998, Lovett et al. 2007).

The California Channel Islands comprise 8 islands located at various distances from the mainland in the Southern California Bight (Figure 1), of which 5 are included in Channel Islands National Park. The islands range in size from less than 300 ha (East Anacapa and Santa Barbara) to over 25,000 ha (Santa Cruz). Of the park islands, East Anacapa is closest to the mainland, being 22 km from the coast, whereas Santa Barbara lies 73 km from the mainland. The larger islands are topographically diverse and support a variety of vegetation habitat types ranging from annual grasslands to coastal scrub communities and oak and conifer woodlands (Halvorson et al. 1988).

Landbirds were selected in the late 1980s as one of the "vital signs" for monitoring the ecological condition or "health" of Channel Island National Park (Davis 1989, Fancy et al. 2009) because they are a conspicuous and important component of the island ecosystems, and are good indicators of changes in the biotic or abiotic components of the environment upon which they depend (Canterbury et al. 2000, Bryce et al. 2002). There is a keen public interest in birds, and birdwatching is a popular recreational pastime that forms the basis for a large and sustainable industry (Sekercioglu 2002). Moreover, numerous species of landbirds can be efficiently surveyed using one basic methodology, and baseline datasets exist for mainland California and throughout the United States to provide context for interpreting the results of the park's monitoring results (Bibby et al. 2000, Buckland et al. 2001).

The California Channel Islands have been the focus of many studies looking at the origin and differentiation, species composition, and turnover among insular avifauna populations (e.g., Diamond 1969, Lynch and Johnson 1974). Breeding land bird communities on the islands are depauperate when compared to those of the mainland. Of the approximately 160 species which breed along the southern California coast, only 44 breed in the park (Diamond and Jones 1980), and the species that breed regularly on the islands are characterized by a high degree of endemism. Thirteen of those species have differentiated into eighteen endemic subspecies (Johnson 1972). Landbird populations in Channel Islands National Park have been historically influenced by past land management practices such as grazing and agriculture, and are currently responding to the recovery of vegetation and other ecological changes that have occurred since the removal of non-native ungulates from the islands.

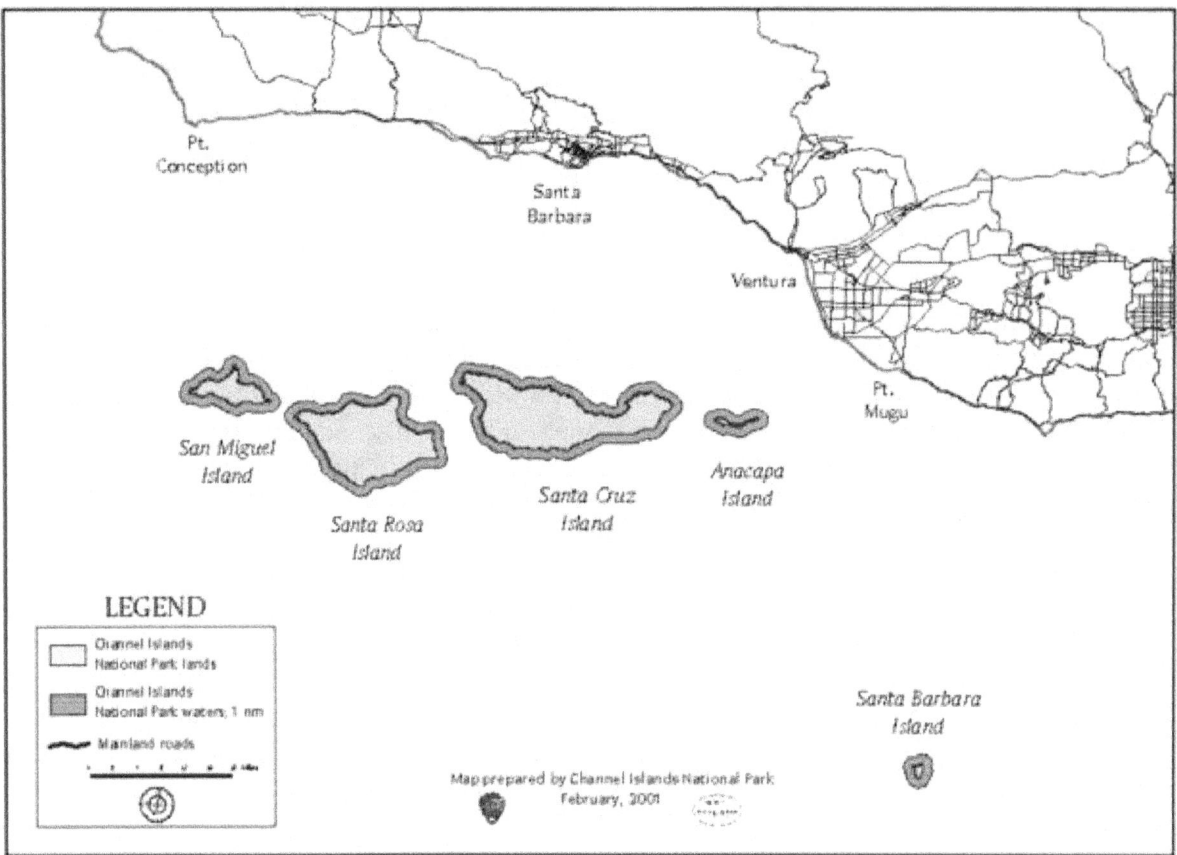

Figure 1. Channel Islands National Park comprises San Miguel, Santa Rosa, Santa Cruz, Anacapa, and Santa Barbara Islands.

History of Landbird Monitoring in Channel Islands National Park

Channel Islands National Park (CHIS) designed and implemented the first long-term ecological monitoring program in the National Park Service, and has more than a 25-year history of providing credible scientific data and information that have been used to inform and support management and planning decisions, and to inform the scientific community, visitors, and various constituency groups about the status and trends in selected park natural resources. The Channel Islands prototype monitoring program was a primary source for much of the early guidance and "best practices" developed by the Servicewide I&M Program, which over the years has produced a long series of "success stories" that demonstrate the value of having an early warning system and long-term data sets to support management decision-making, planning, education, and research (Fancy et al. 2009). In October 1988, three NPS scientists with the Cooperative Parks Studies Unit -- Charles van Riper III, Mark Sogge and Charles Drost -- provided the park with a monitoring protocol to assist resource managers with "assessing changes in relative population levels of land birds" (van Riper et al. 1988). A modification of this protocol was implemented on three of the park's five islands in 1993, and since then the park has used the same basic approach to monitor landbirds in the park each year.

Beginning in 1993, line transect surveys using distance sampling were conducted at approximately the same time of year each spring and fall on 3 transects on Santa Barbara, 1 transect on East Anacapa, and 5 transects on San Miguel island. The annual landbird surveys in the fall have not been conducted since 1998 because of funding and staffing constraints. In 1994, the park began monitoring landbirds on Santa Rosa Island using a protocol developed by Super et al. (1991) that involved a series of 11 transects using 50-m fixed radius point counts and four line transects where distance estimation was used.

In April 2000, a formal technical review of the landbird monitoring program at Channel Islands National Park was undertaken by eight bird monitoring experts (McEachern 2000). As described in more detail in Chapter 2.2 below, the review team recommended that the park switch to a new spatially-structured, stratified random design to estimate landbird abundance on the five islands in the park, and that the old (1993-2000) and new (2001 onwards) sampling sites both be sampled over a three-year transition period to provide a crosswalk between the two data sets. Because of funding and staffing constraints, the full transition to the new sampling design, which involved establishing the new sampling sites and conducting monitoring at both the old and new sites for at least three years, was not fully completed until 2008. This protocol was written in 2011 to document the landbird monitoring methods conducted since 1993 and to formalize the methods that are now used to monitor landbirds on the five islands in the park.

Measurable Objectives

This monitoring program was designed to inform managers and other stakeholders at Channel Islands National Park about long-term changes in the composition, abundance, and distribution of landbird species and assemblages of species. The specific measurable objectives of the landbird monitoring efforts that relate to park information needs and management are as follows:

1. Determine long-term trends in species composition, distribution, and abundance of native and non-native landbird species in selected areas of Channel Islands National Park.

2. Improve our understanding of breeding bird – habitat relationships and the effects of management actions such as alien plant and animal control on bird populations by correlating changes in landbird species composition, distribution, and abundance with changes in specific habitat variables.

Ideally, we would estimate trends in abundance and distribution for all species each year on each of the five islands in the park, and compare these estimates with comparable data for areas on the California mainland to provide context. Such a goal, however, is unachievable due to numerous practical and logistical constraints, including the steep and unsafe terrain that occurs in many areas of the islands, the high cost and difficulty of working on the islands, the diversity of ecological communities, and the large number of species that occur in the park. To meet these challenges, we have tried to design a program that maximizes the strength of our inferences within the context of our finite resources. Our program provides a multi-tiered, flexible framework that will enable efficient estimation and monitoring of population parameters, periodic evaluation of assumptions, and the opportunity to adapt the program to meet additional needs.

2. Sampling Design

2.1 Rationale for Selecting this Sampling Design over Others

This protocol uses line transect sampling and point-transect surveys (also known as Variable Circular Plot [VCP] counts) to produce island-specific and species-specific estimates of landbird abundance and patterns of bird distribution. Distance sampling has been used for more than 30 years to estimate animal abundance (Reynolds et al. 1980; Nelson and Fancy 1999; Buckland et al. 2001, 2004; Rosenstock et al. 2002), and is a very common approach for landbird monitoring because numerous species can be monitored using the same basic approach. Distance sampling designs provide better estimates of species abundance and trends when compared to traditional point-count techniques (Ralph et al. 1995) because they make it possible to estimate the probability of detecting a particular species (i.e., detection probability). Estimating the distance to each bird allows density to be approximated via a species-specific detection function that accounts for variation in detectability due to observer, habitat type, or weather-related factors (Buckland et al. 2001, 2004; Diefenbach et al. 2003). Our use of distance sampling will provide data that are comparable among islands, and will also facilitate comparisons with data from national parks and other locations in North America where the same survey methods are used. The field methods described in this protocol will also allow us to compare our results to other monitoring efforts such as the Breeding Bird Survey (BBS).

In the case of line transect sampling, the observer walks down a transect and records either the perpendicular distance to each bird heard or seen, or else records the sighting angle and sighting distance instead of the perpendicular distance. Variable circular plots are a type of distance sampling in which the observer stands at a sampling station and records the horizontal distances to each bird detected. Line transects are usually more efficient than VCP counts where they can be conducted because data are collected continually as an observer walks down the transect, whereas during VCP counts birds are counted only at stations located along the transect. VCP counts are the preferred approach in patchy habitats if the goal is to associate bird data with vegetation or other habitat information, and in dense, rugged or hazardous terrain where an observer needs to watch their footing. Another advantage of VCP counts is that the data can be directly compared to historical point count data such as from BBS counts and can contribute to ongoing programs such as the National Point Count Database.

Provided that assumptions are reasonably met, distance-sampling allows researchers to model a detection function that adjusts for imperfect detectability, and is a robust, widely accepted method for estimating abundance of landbirds (Buckland et al. 2001, 2004). With reasonable effort, we will likely be able to estimate density annually for most of the common landbird species in the park. Annual estimates of density for less-common species will also be possible by pooling data across multiple years. Although distance sampling generally does improve estimates of abundance and population trends for many species, it is not a panacea and there are a number of limitations of the method even with the best trained and most highly skilled observers (e.g., Simons et al. 2009).

2.2 Selection of Sampling Sites and Timing of Surveys

The original landbird monitoring protocol developed for Channel Islands National Park (van Riper et al. 1988) was designed to monitor relative abundance of populations of landbird species which breed on Santa Barbara, East Anacapa and San Miguel Islands through the use of line transect sampling during both the breeding and non-breeding seasons. Line transects utilizing existing trail systems were chosen over point counts because they minimize impact to vegetation while accurately sampling avian species composition, relative abundance and seasonal distribution patterns (Sogge et al. 1989). The landbird monitoring program developed for Santa Rosa Island (Super et al. 1991) primarily utilized point count sampling which was more appropriate for that island's structurally complex habitats and rugged terrain, both of which make line transect sampling difficult to implement.

A formal technical review of the landbird monitoring program at Channel Islands National Park was conducted in April 2000 by eight bird monitoring experts (McEachern 2000). The objectives of the review were as follows:

- Determine whether the monitoring protocol is achieving the park's objectives for its monitoring program;
- Identify the level of temporal change that can be detected with the existing protocol and the level of confidence in detecting change;
- Identify opportunities and techniques to improve power and efficiency of monitoring;
- Accommodate improvements in technology (such as data collection technology, GPS, database management software), as appropriate, into the protocols; and
- Foster the cross-linking of protocols and integration across monitoring programs to help the Park better understand ecosystem dynamics.

One of the key management questions for the park was to determine how bird populations were responding to changes in vegetation and other environmental factors as the islands recovered from the detrimental effects of past land use practices. To better address this key management question, the review team recommended that the park switch to a new spatially-structured, stratified random design to estimate landbird abundance on all five islands in the park. The team recommended that the old and new sampling sites both be sampled over a three-year transition period to provide a crosswalk between the old (1993-2000) and new (2001 onwards) data sets. Based on an analysis of data collected during 1993-2000, the review team recommended that the park continue to monitor landbirds in the park annually, but recommended that the fall sampling season be discontinued because of funding and staffing constraints so that adequate time is available for data entry, analysis, and reporting of the annual monitoring results.

The locations of the original line transects and the new point count sampling stations that were selected based on the recommendations from the technical review in 2000 are shown in Figures 2 through 13 below. A complete listing of site locations is provided in SOP #3. On the three smaller islands, the new sites were randomly selected using a GIS application with a minimum spacing of 250 m between stations. This resulted in 8 sites on East Anacapa Island and 33 sites on Santa Barbara Island. Due to park and island logistics, it is feasible to sample both these new sites as well as the line transects that have been sampled since 1993. On San Miguel Island, 40 random sites were selected, with a denser concentration of sites on the more accessible eastern side of the island, and a lower density of sites on the less accessible western side of the island. The goal on San Miguel, with its often windy and foggy spring mornings, is to complete the point transect surveys each spring, and to also sample the line transects that have been sampled since 1993 if time and staffing allow. Habitat type at each point count site was determined by ocular estimation of approximate percent cover (Table SOP 3-1). Of the 8 East Anacapa Island sites, 5 were in habitat types dominated by Coreopsis, 2 in grassland, and 1 dominated by introduced ice plant. The dominant habitat types for the 33 Santa Barbara Island sites are 17 grassland, 5 Coreopsis, 4 seablite scrub, 3 ice plant, 1 boxthorn scrub, and 1 seacliff scrub. On San Miguel Island, site habitat types were 11 grassland, 8 lupine, 8 Coreopsis, 5 coastal scrub, 3 coastal sage scrub, 2 caliche scrub, 1 baccharis scrub, 1 coastal bluff scrub, 1 riparian herbaceous, and 1 riparian woodland.

On the much larger Santa Rosa Island, the review team recommended using a sampling scheme stratified by ease of access (near-road and off-road), with sampling stations clustered in groups of 3 to 5 stations to reduce the travel time between points and allow for a more efficient design. Roads considered for near-road sites included relatively permanent "blue roads" that the park expects to maintain after 2011 when the park gains full control of the island ("red" closed roads and "green" roads may not be accessible after 2011). Selected sampling sites were randomly weighted to include most habitat types, and any sites on steep slopes that were unsafe to sample were excluded. The GIS analysis resulted in 82 random near-road stations being selected where the transect started less than 100 m from the road, and 63 off-road stations selected for sites where the transect begins more than 100 m from a maintained road. Dominant habitat types included 37 coastal sage scrub, 30 grassland, 30 chaparral, 9 mixed woodland, 8 riparian, 6 closed cone pine, 6 Torrey pine, 6 oak woodland, 5 lupine, 4 riparian herbaceous, and 4 riparian woodland.

Landbird monitoring stations are marked with 2-foot high aluminum stakes in very low vegetation, and 4-foot high aluminum stakes elsewhere. In most sites, the aluminum site marker stakes were placed so that they are not readily visible to visitors and the markers were painted to blend in with the vegetation. Some transects were grouped into numbered units, each unit being the most likely number of stations that can be counted during one morning, taking into account travel time by foot between stations and by vehicle between transects. These units can be surveyed in any order, depending on what is most convenient at the time. If road or trail closures are implemented on the island, it may be necessary to re-evaluate the sampling scheme.

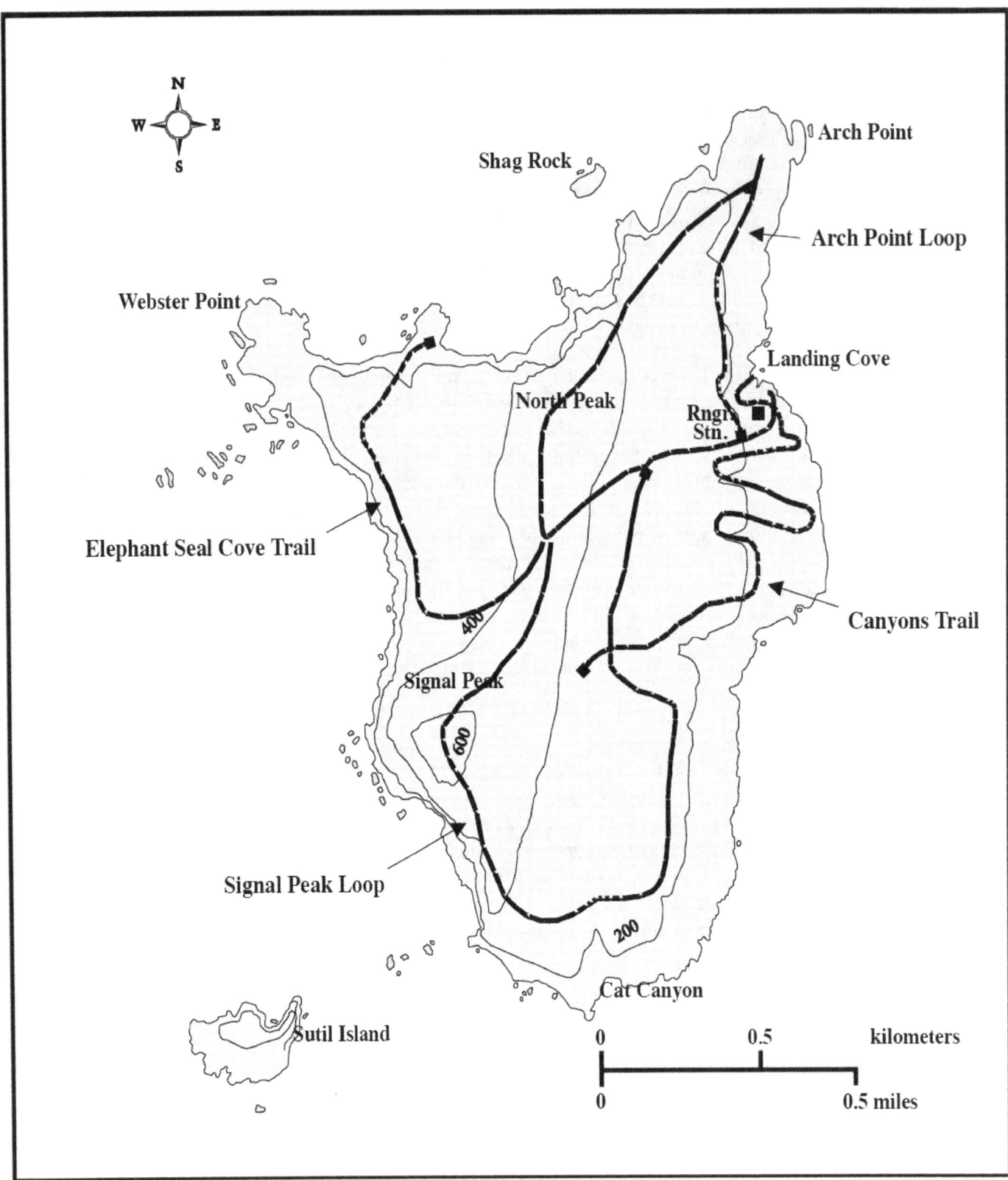

Figure 2. Landbird transect locations on Santa Barbara Island, Channel Islands National Park.

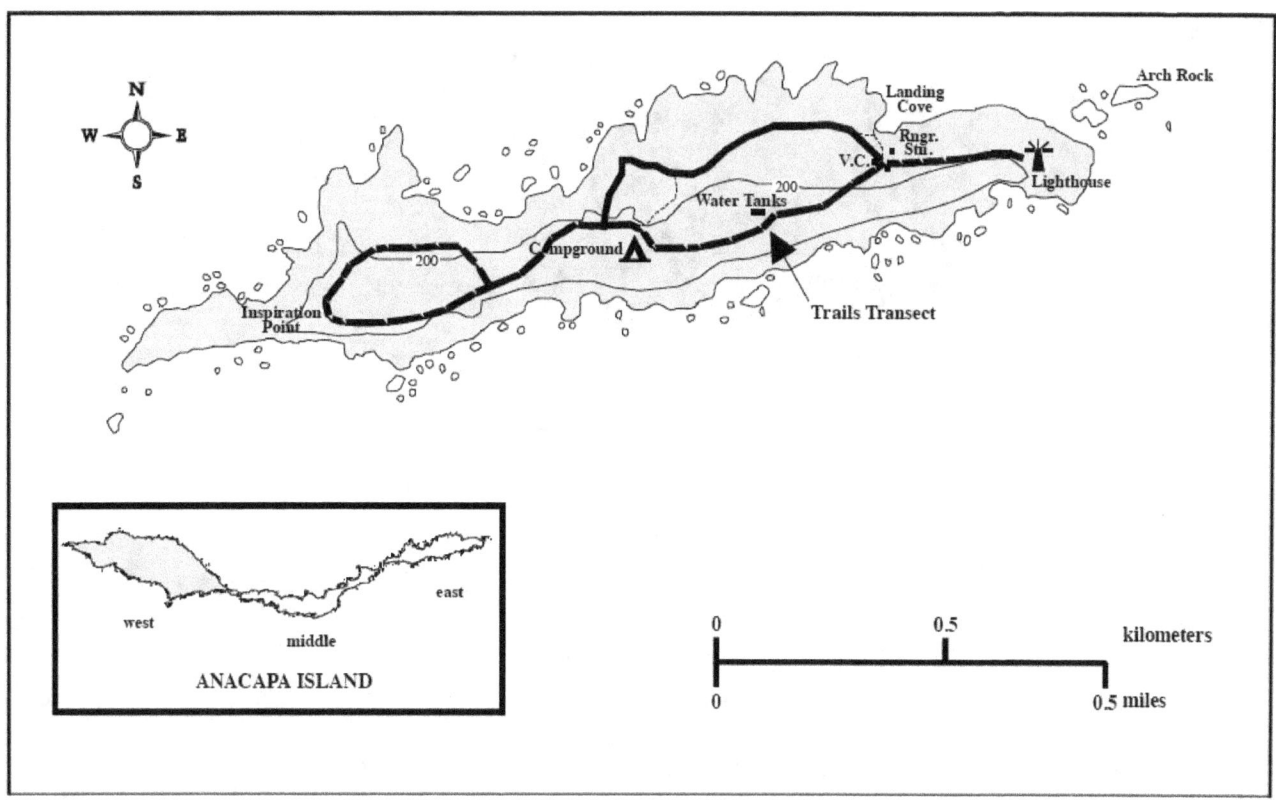

Figure 3. Landbird transect locations on East Anacapa Island, Channel Islands National Park.

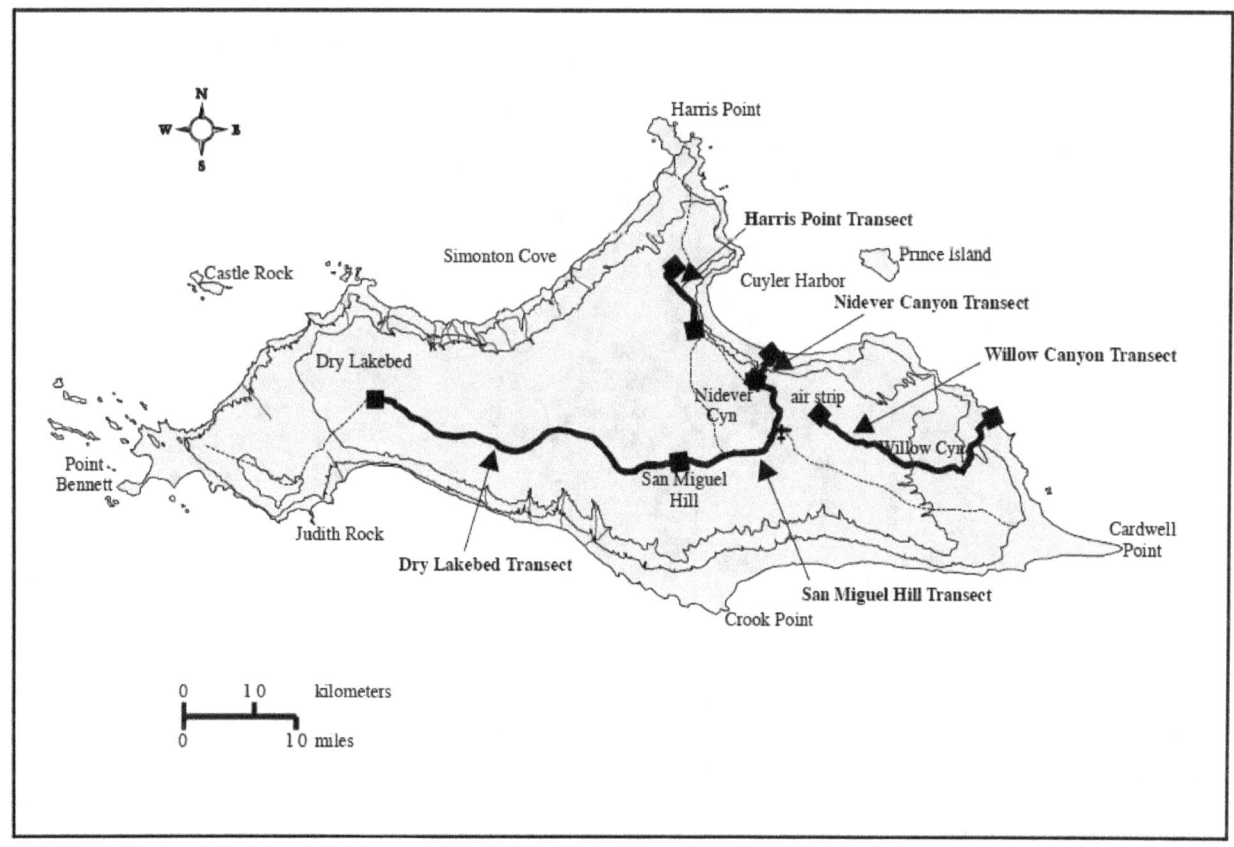

Figure 4. Landbird transect locations on San Miguel Island, Channel Islands National Park.

9

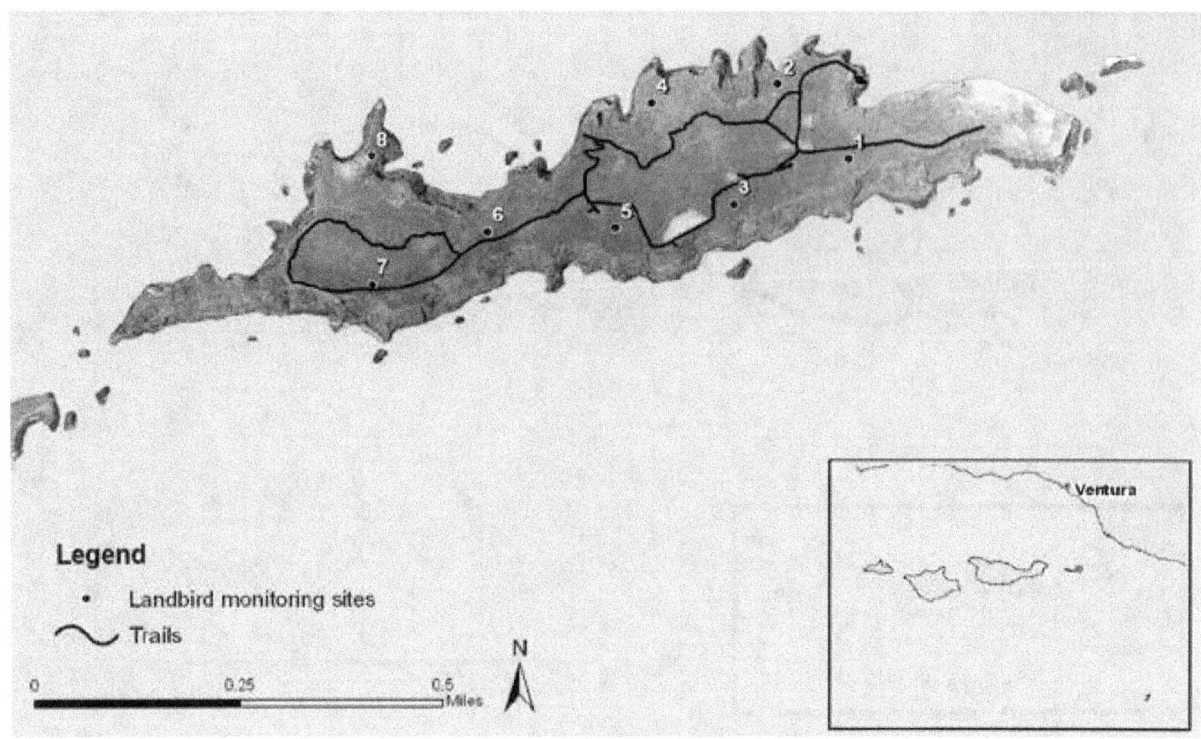

Figure 5. Location of landbird point count monitoring sites on East Anacapa Island.

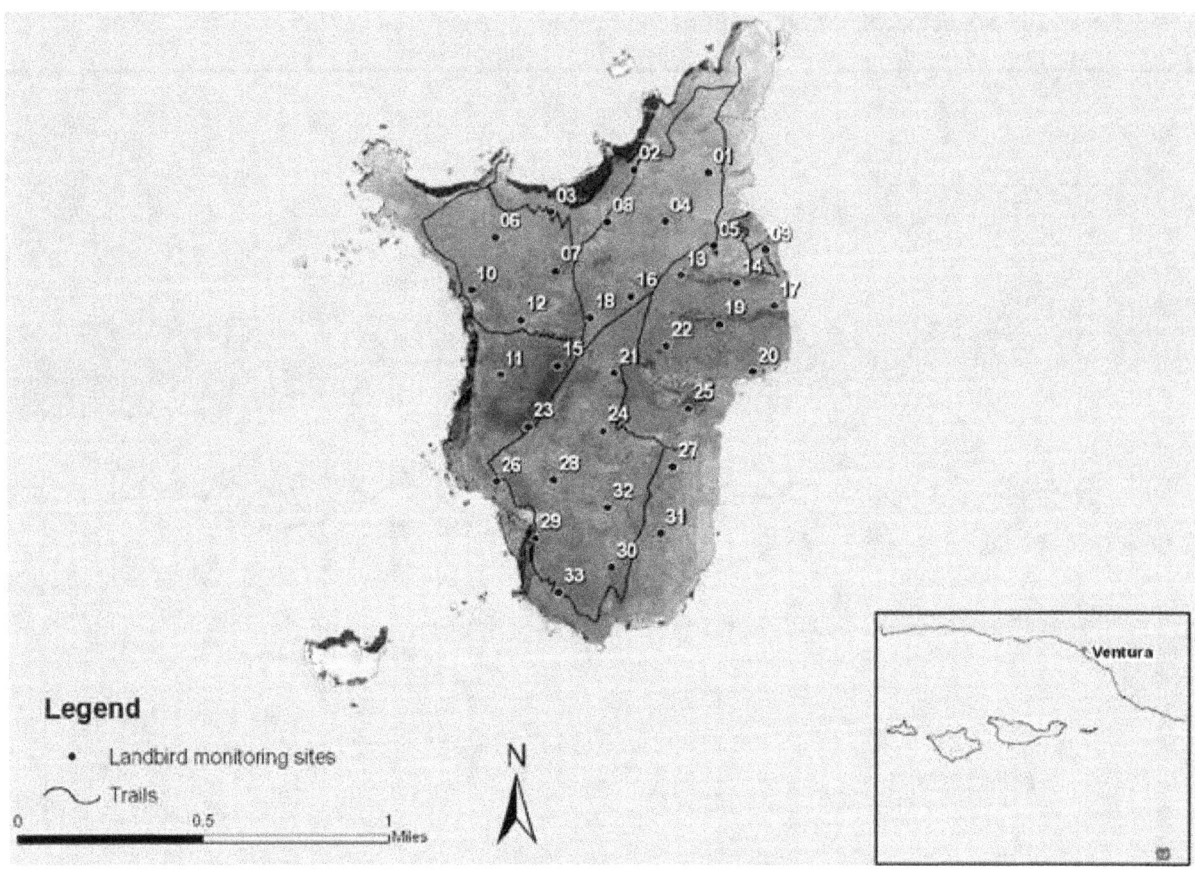

Figure 6. Location of landbird point count monitoring sites on Santa Barbara Island.

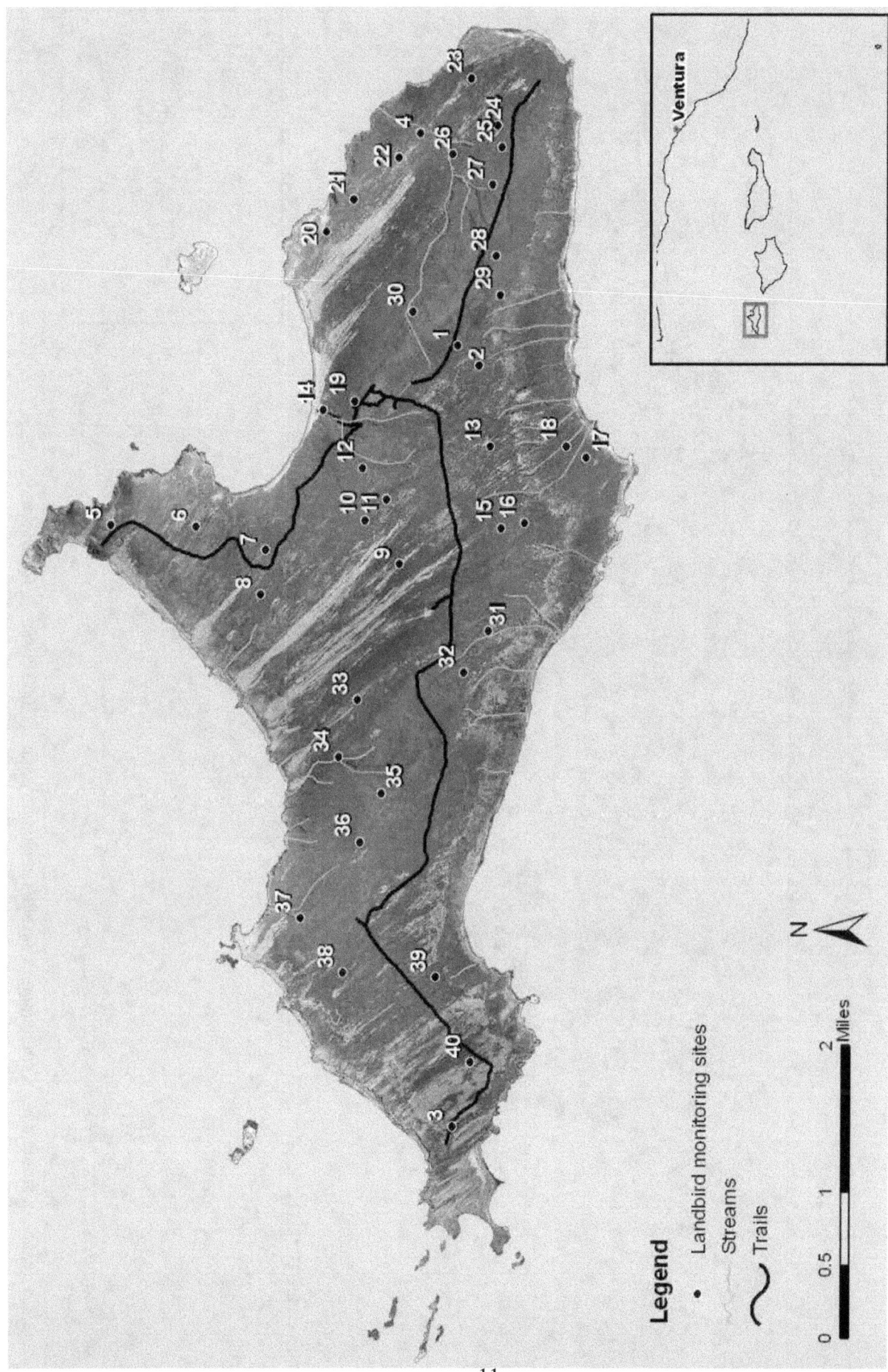

Figure 7. Location of landbird point count monitoring sites on San Miguel Island.

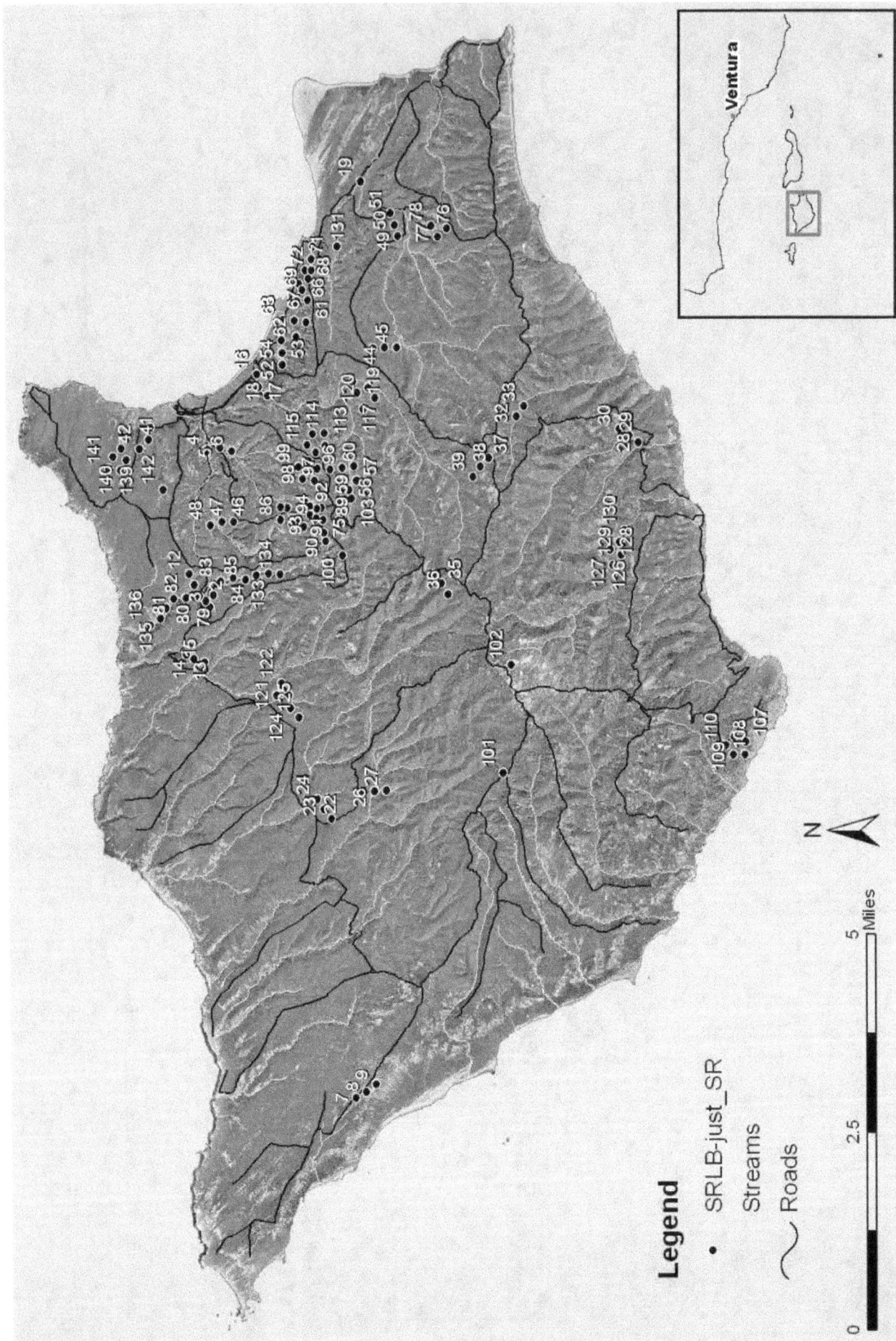

Figure 8. Location of landbird point count monitoring sites implemented after 2000 on Santa Rosa Island.

Legend

• SRLB-just_SR

Streams

Roads

N

0   2.5   5
Miles

Ventura

Santa Rosa Island Landbird Monitoring Sites

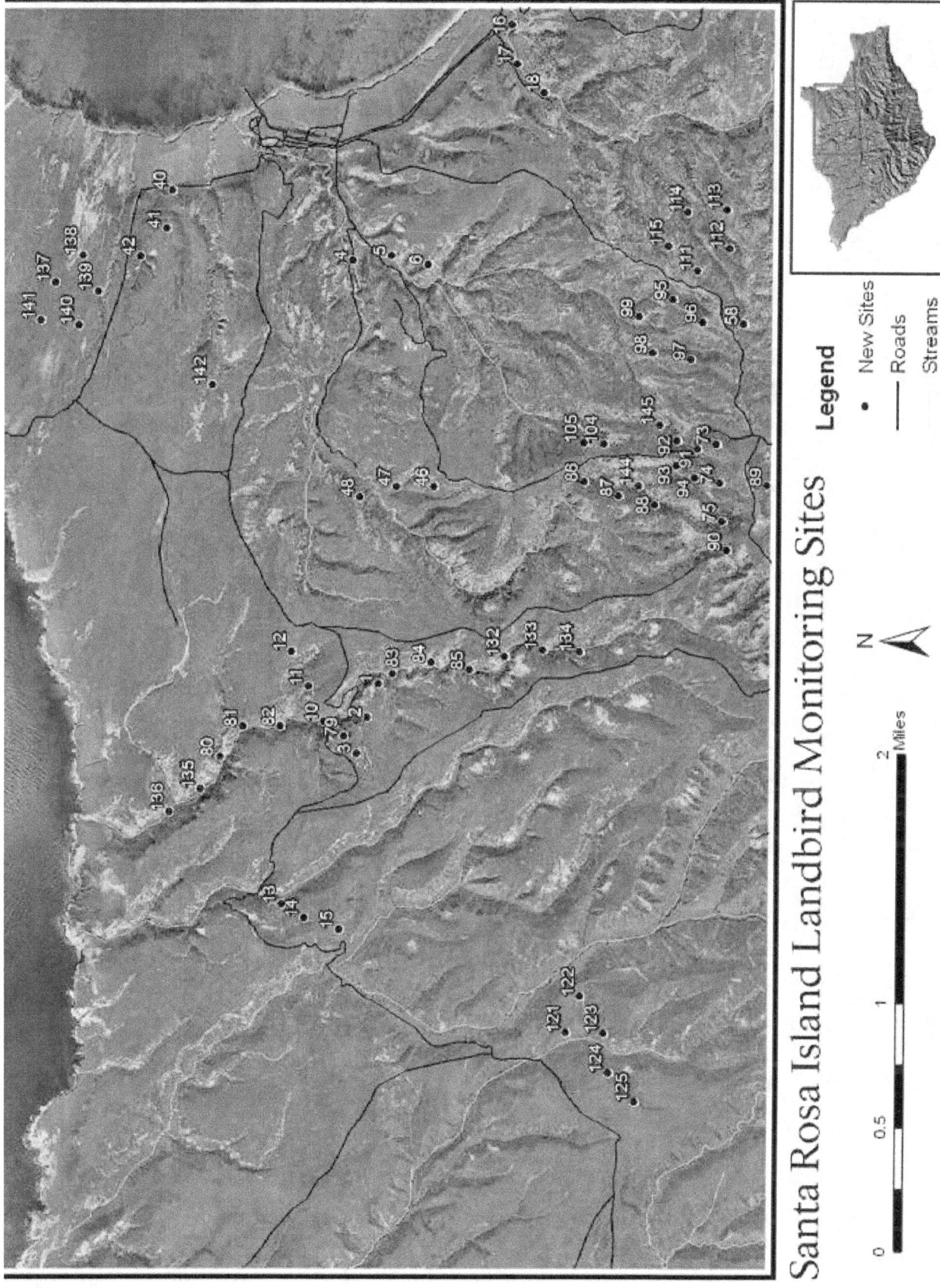

Legend

• New Sites
— Roads
   Streams

N

Miles

0   0.5   1   2

Figure 9. Location of landbird point count monitoring sites on northeast Santa Rosa Island.

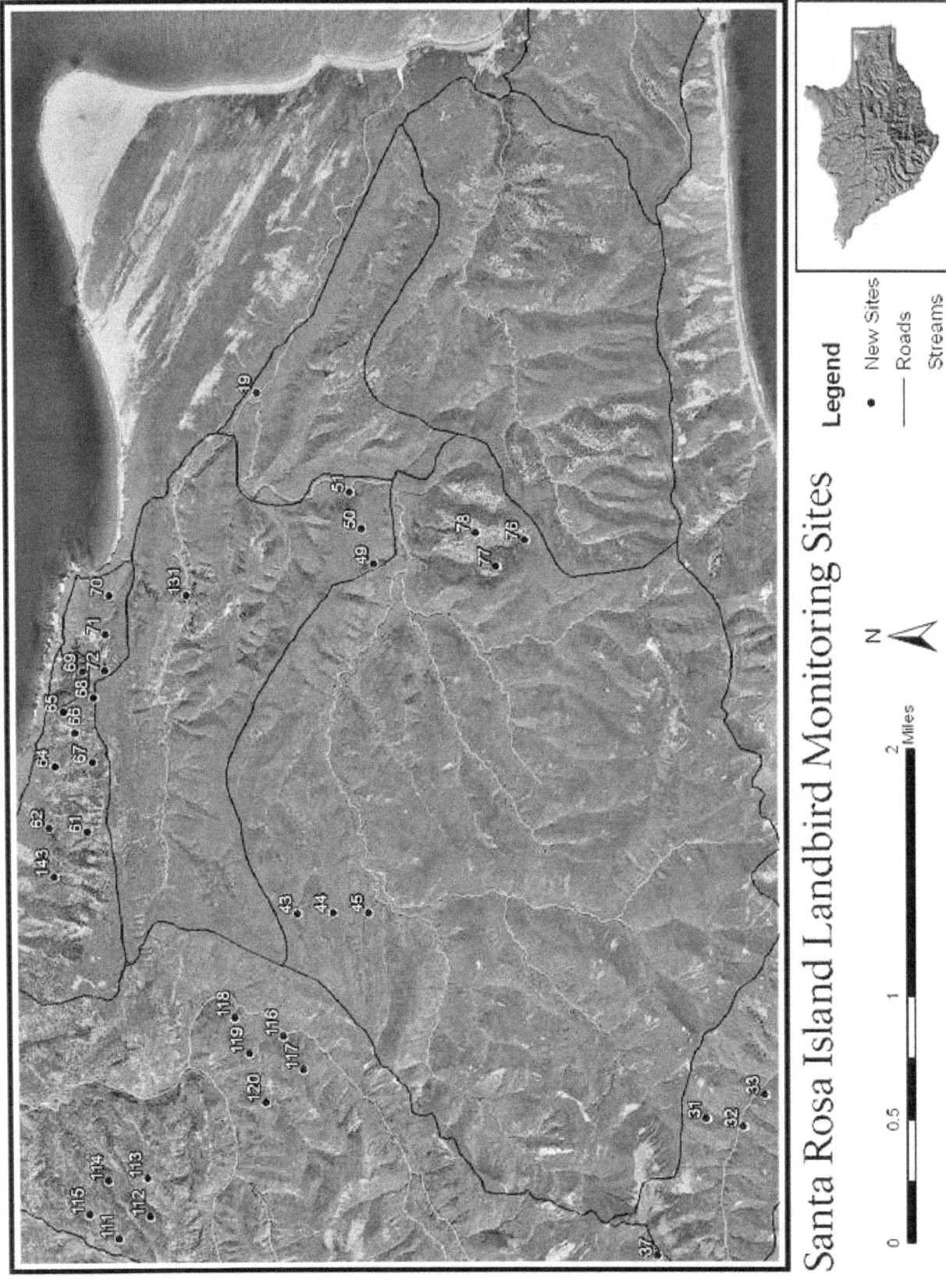

Santa Rosa Island Landbird Monitoring Sites

Legend
• New Sites
— Roads
   Streams

Figure 10. Location of landbird point count monitoring sites on east Santa Rosa Island.

14

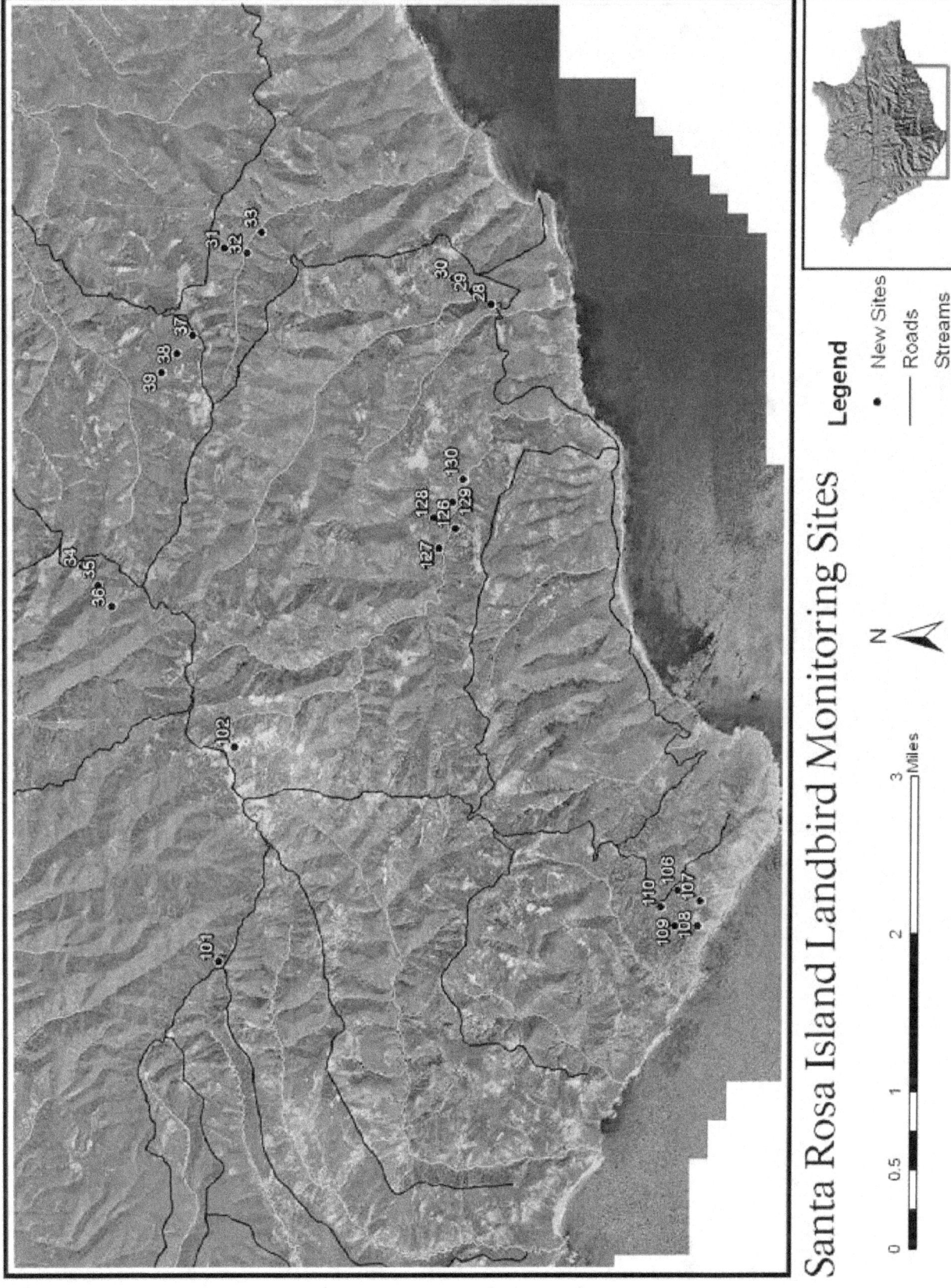

Santa Rosa Island Landbird Monitoring Sites

Legend

- New Sites
- —— Roads
- Streams

N

0   0.5   1   2   3
Miles

Figure 11. Location of landbird point count monitoring sites on the south side of Santa Rosa Island.

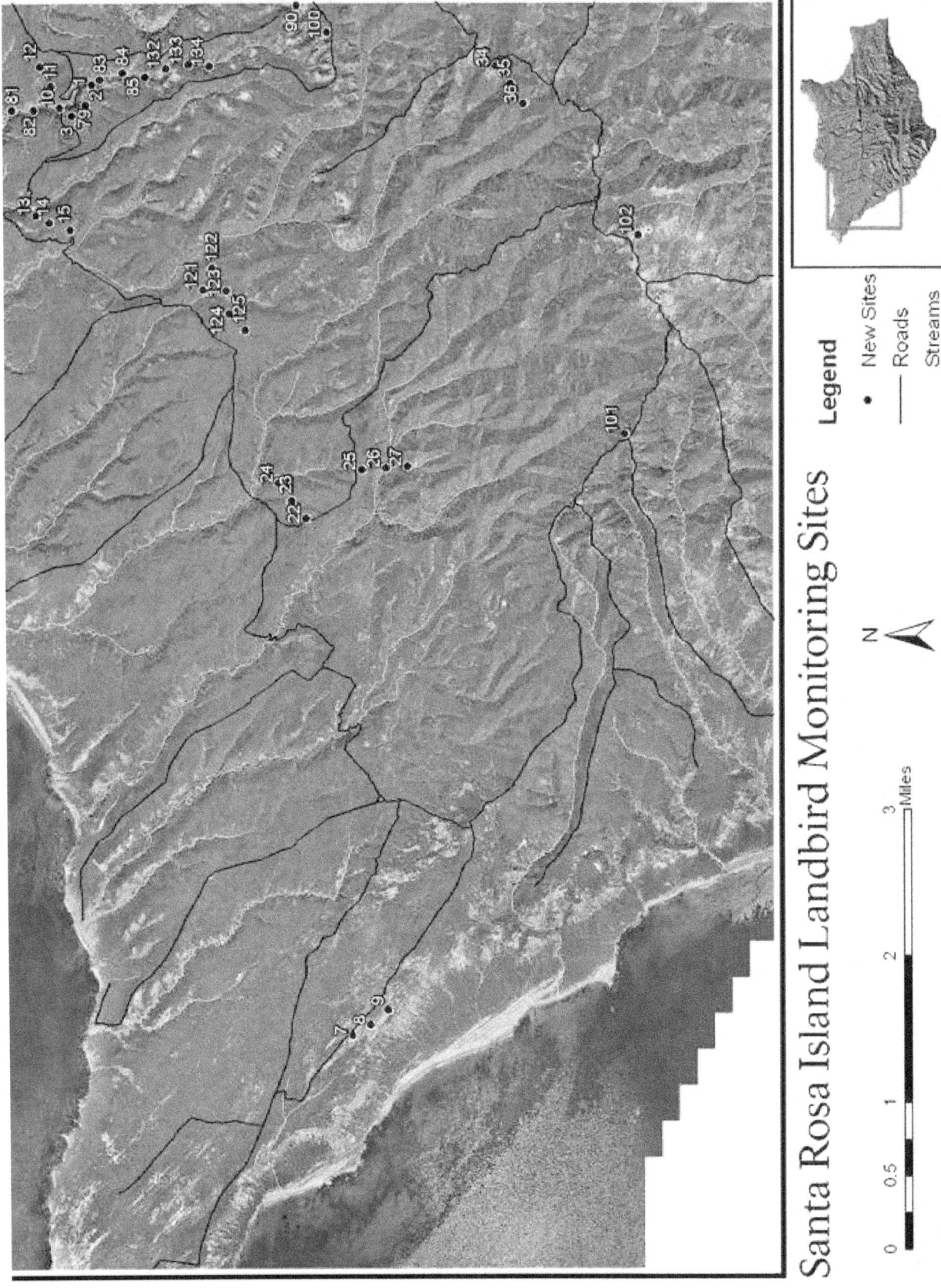

Santa Rosa Island Landbird Monitoring Sites

Legend

- New Sites
— Roads
— Streams

N

0   0.5   1   2   3
Miles

Figure 12. Location of landbird point count monitoring sites on west Santa Rosa Island.

3. Field Methods

3.1 Field Season Preparations and Field Schedule

Prior to each field season, observers will read the entire protocol narrative and all standard operating procedures (SOPs). Observers should pay special attention to the field tasks described in SOPs #2, #4, and #5. Practice and training in identifying birds by sight and sound is critical; the misidentification of a species is the most serious error one can make during counts (Kepler and Scott 1981, Royle and Link 2006). Observers should also review estimation of distances to birds detected. All equipment and supplies listed in SOP #1 should be organized and made ready for the field season. Observers should review the alphabetical codes for each species typically seen during spring sampling on each island.

Unpredictable weather and the logistical difficulties of working on islands that can only be accessed by boat or airplane necessitate maintaining flexibility in scheduling the sequence and duration of sampling events during each field season. Breeding bird surveys will be conducted during the period that coincides with the peak-breeding activity of most birds (March through June, starting in March for the southern islands; Table 1). Specific survey dates may vary slightly because of weather, boat schedules, island road conditions and other island conditions. Santa Barbara and East Anacapa Islands can be sampled in one tour by one observer. San Miguel Island can usually be sampled by two observers in one tour depending on fog and wind conditions. Santa Rosa Island sampling requires two observers for up to six tours, depending on weather and road conditions. The sampling dates will be documented in a tour summary for each tour/event group before leaving the island with notes on unusual events.

Table 2. Annual field schedule for landbird monitoring at Channel Islands National Park.

Island	Survey Date Interval
Santa Barbara	Early March
East Anacapa	Early to mid-March
San Miguel	Mid-March to early June
Santa Rosa	Mid-March to early June

3.2 Conducting Point-Count and Line Transect Surveys

The detailed instructions for conducting the surveys and properly filling out the field data form are provided in SOP #5 for point counts and SOP #6 for line transects, and are summarized here. For point counts, sampling will occur in the morning, beginning as soon as it is light enough to see a distance of at least 400 m and ending no later than 4 hours after official sunrise. Observers should arrive at the first plot while it is still dark so that the count can begin as soon as it is light enough to see. Singing rate for most species is usually highest before or near official sunrise and then declines slowly for the next four hours. Counts should not be conducted during high winds or heavy rains because these conditions inhibit bird activity and impair the ability to see and hear birds. Counts should not be conducted if wind strength on the Beaufort scale is a sustained 4 or greater (see Table SOP 5-1), or if it is raining hard or snowing (rain code >4 in Table SOP 5-2). Observers encountering these conditions should wait until the weather improves or postpone sampling until another day.

Observers should strive for the most accurate count possible, not the largest count, and the protocol should be adhered to strictly. Birds should not be counted unless their identification is certain. The survey at each point should be a "snapshot" in time, and the results should represent the actual distribution of the birds relative to the point. Some movement of birds into and out of the plot is acceptable, as long as a bird is only counted once and the observer does not cause movement. The most important birds to detect are those very close to the observer (within 20 m of the point), and it is highly desirable that estimated distances be within 1 to 2 m of actual distances for all birds detected within that radius. However, all birds seen or heard should be recorded with an estimate of distance measured with a laser rangefinder. Rounding distances to the nearest 5 or 10 m is discouraged unless accurate distance estimation is not possible because of vegetation or topography.

Observers should approach the plot vigilantly, and if a bird observed close to the center of the plot flushes as a result of an approaching observer, that bird should be counted and the initial distance from the plot center to that bird should be recorded on the data form. This is because a critical assumption of the distance methodology is that any bird directly at (or very close to, e.g., <5-10 m from the) the plot center will always be detected, i.e., $g(0) = 1$ (Buckland et al. 2001, 2004). The observer should set a watch or timer for 10 minutes, and once the count has begun, all birds heard or seen during the ten minutes should be recorded, regardless of their distance from the center of the point. By recording the time that each bird was detected and comparing it to the starting time, there will be a record of how many birds were detected during the first three minutes of the count (for comparisons with raw counts from Breeding Bird Survey data), during the first five minutes (for comparison with data from the mainland that uses that time interval), and for the full ten minutes.

For each bird heard or seen, the observer records the horizontal distance in meters between the point center (where the observer is standing), and the location of the bird where it was first detected. Distances should be estimated to the nearest meter; do not round off to the nearest five meters. If the bird is detected aurally (call or song) but not visually, distance should be estimated to some object (such as a tree, bush, or rock) near where the bird is located. If the bird flies into the observer's field of vision and then lands nearby, distance should be recorded to where it was first observed and not to where it landed. For species that occur in clusters or flocks, distance should be recorded from the observer to the center of the flock. If a bird is high in a tree, the observer should imagine dropping a plumb bob from the bird down to the ground, and estimate the horizontal distance to that spot on the ground. Flyovers (birds that fly above the top of the vegetation canopy, never touch down, and do not appear to be foraging, displaying, or behaving in any other way that might suggest a link to the habitat below them) should be recorded by entering -9999 in the distance column. For each bird, the cue by which the bird was first detected (call, song or visual) is recorded.

The methods and the field data form for line transects are similar in many ways to those for point counts. Each transect is walked at a moderately slow, steady pace and for all birds seen or heard, the observer records the perpendicular distance (to the nearest meter) between the transect midline and the bird. The observer should pause only to confirm identification of a bird, and should record all detections of landbird species seen or heard on either side of the trail. As with point counts, the cue by which the bird was first detected (call, song or visual) is recorded for each bird. Observers count only those birds detected in the area directly to the sides of or in front of the observer; birds detected behind the observer are not counted, and no birds are counted twice. Birds may be counted if they are on the ground, in vegetation, or in flight, and flying birds may be counted at any height. If the bird cannot be seen, distance should nonetheless be estimated, but if a reasonable distance estimate cannot be made, the bird should not be counted. Use of laser range finders can greatly assist in distance estimation.

After the conclusion of the point count or line transect, the observer reviews the data form and fills in all fields on the data form before departing for the next sampling point or line transect. Also, the observer should search the area to ensure that no equipment is left behind. Any observations of other notable plant and animal species before, during, or after the landbird counts should be recorded on the separate "Incidental Observations" data form (see Figure SOP 5-2).

4. Data Management, Analysis, and Reporting

The following section outlines general procedures for data handling, analysis, and report development. Additional details and context for this chapter may be found in the Data Management Plan and SOPs for the Mediterranean Coast I&M Network (MEDN). The MEDN monitoring plan also provides a good overview of the Network's information management and reporting plan. It is crucial that project personnel know and understand their responsibilities in implementing data management methods and the timelines they are expected to follow when conducting data management.

4.1 Overview of Database Design
The Microsoft Access database for the Channel Island National Park landbird monitoring protocol is compliant with the Natural Resource Database Template standards (Version 3) adopted by the national I&M program. We modified a database developed by Kristen Beaupre for the Sonoran Desert I&M Network, which included data structures and features developed by John Boetsch of the North Coast and Cascades I&M Network. The back-end data structure and many of the features of the database are common to several I&M networks within the National Park Service, which will facilitate future sharing and comparing of data and data analysis routines.

The database includes three files: the *LB.mdb* front-end file, *LB_BE.mdb* back-end file, and *LB_Master_Bird_List.be.mdb* file that are linked using the Backend Linking Utility in the database. The front-end file, *LB.mdb*, acts as the user interface into the back-end database and contains the forms, queries, reports, and VBA code for the application. *LB_ be.mdb*, the back-end file, contains the data tables. This configuration facilitates improvements and revisions to the database front-end application without altering the actual data structure or any of the records in the back-end data tables.

The primary table for storing bird detection data (tbl_Detections) contains observation information such as species, distance from observer, time of detection, age, sex, and flock size. Supporting tables include data for the location (e.g., location ID, coordinates, habitat type, elevation) and event (date, time, observers, version of the protocol that was being followed, weather conditions during the count). Species, observer names and other contact information, and attribute look-up tables provide standardized values for many data fields.

4.2 Data Entry, Verification and Validation
The Project Manger is responsible for making sure all datasheets are complete and accurate and that data is entered properly into the database. The database has a user-friendly interface to

facilitate data entry and checking (verification). Data verification is the process of ensuring the data entered into a database correspond with the data recorded on the hardcopy field forms. Once the data have been entered and saved, the Project Manager and MEDN Data Manager will validate the data by reviewing the data for quality, completeness, and logical consistency. Data validation requires a reviewer to have extensive knowledge of what the data mean and how they were collected. Queries and reports have been built to look for apparent outliers, inconsistencies in entry, null values, or any other anomalous data points. Anomalies are reported to the Project Manager for resolution. Unresolved anomalies will be documented and included in the metadata and certification report. Any questions about the data, data entry procedures, or difficulties with the database are to be resolved by the Project Manager and MEDN Data Manager.

Once all verification and validation methods have been implemented, the working database will be transferred to the MEDN Data Manager, who will upload them to the master database. While uploading the data to the database, the data will be subjected to an automated data quality process that will flag potential missing sites and invalid or improperly formatted data.

4.3 Data Certification and Delivery

Data certification is a benchmark in the project information management process that indicates that 1) the data are complete for the period of record; 2) they have undergone and passed the quality assurance checks; and 3) that they are appropriately documented and in a condition for archiving, posting, and distribution. Certification is not intended to imply that the data are completely free of errors or inconsistencies which may not have been detected during quality assurance reviews. Rather, it describes a formal and standardized process to track and minimize errors.

To ensure that only data of the highest possible quality are included in reports and other project deliverables, the data certification step is an annual requirement for all tabular and spatial data. The Project Manager is primarily responsible for completing certification. The completed form, certified data, and updated metadata should be delivered to the MEDN Data Manager according to the specified timeline.

4.4 Metadata Procedures

Data documentation is a critical step toward ensuring that datasets are useable for their intended purposes well into the future. This involves the development of metadata, which can be defined as structured information about the content, quality, and condition of data. Additionally, metadata provide the means to catalog datasets within intranet and internet systems, making data more accessible to a broad range of potential users. Metadata for all MEDN monitoring data will conform to Federal Geographic Data Committee (FGDC) and NPS guidelines and will contain all components of supporting information such that the data may be confidently manipulated, analyzed, and synthesized. For long-term projects such as this one, metadata creation is most time consuming the first time it is developed – after which most information remains static from one year to the next. Metadata records in subsequent years then only need to be updated to reflect current publications, references, taxonomic conventions, contact information, data disposition and quality, and to describe any changes in collection methods, analysis approaches or quality assurance for the project.

Specific procedures for metadata development and posting are outlined in the MEDN Data Management Plan. In general, the Project Lead and MEDN Data Manager will work together to create and update an FGDC- and NPS-compliant metadata record in XML format. The Project Manager should update the metadata content as changes to the protocol are made, and each year as additional data are accumulated. Edits within the document should be tracked so that any changes are obvious to those who will use it to update the XML metadata file. The MEDN Data Manager will facilitate metadata development by creating and parsing metadata records, and by posting such records to the NPS IRMA (Integrated Resource Management Applications) data system where they will be available to the public.

4.5 Sensitive Information

Part of metadata development includes determining whether or not the data include any sensitive information, which includes specific locations of rare, threatened, or endangered species. Prior to completing metadata, the Project Manager and Park Resource Manager should work together to identify any sensitive information in the data. Their findings should be documented and communicated to MEDN Data Manager.

4.6 Data Archival

File structure, version control, and regular backups are carefully controlled to preserve the integrity of MEDN datasets. Field datasheets are copied and scanned as they come in from the islands. Copies of field data sheets will be stored in designated file cabinets at each network park. After field datasheets have been entered into the database with any associated corrections or notes, these datasheets will be scanned into PDF documents, stored in the project directory on the server. The original datasheets along with an archival quality DVD containing all data and trip reports/metadata for that year will be sent to park archive storage. After all data for a field season have been entered, verified, validated, and certified by the Project Manager, the database will be sent to the MEDN Data Manager for archival and distribution. The archived database will be stored on a secure server with regularly scheduled back-ups and will be read-only accessible to the network parks. A complete copy of the database also will be archived prior to any database version changes. Once the data have been archived, any changes made to data values must be documented in the edit log database table. Once a dateset is archived, paper field data sheets will not be altered; field data will be reconciled to the database through the use of the edit log. Any editing of archived datasets will be accomplished jointly by the Project Manager and MEDN Data Manager.

Certified and archived non-sensitive data, along with any associated metadata, will be made available through the NPS IRMA data system at http://irma.nps.gov. The MEDN Data Manager will post certified datasets to IRMA where they may be downloaded for research and management applications. Other datasets, including those containing sensitive data, may be requested in writing from the Project Manager. Sensitive data will be released only with a signed confidentiality agreement.

4.6 Routine Data Summaries and Statistical Analyses to Detect Trends

The detailed procedures for analyzing data and producing routine data summaries, annual reports, and occasional trend reports, are described in SOP #8 (Data Summary, Analysis, and Reporting), and SOP #9 (Data Analysis using Program DISTANCE). These procedures are expected to change more frequently than will the field methods or overall approach for the monitoring, as improved methods for analyzing, graphing, and reporting the monitoring results are developed by NPS I&M networks and their partners throughout the nation.

Standardized data summary routines are built into the *LB.mdb* database to streamline the process for routine production of annual reports and for exporting data to the R statistical package and to the DISTANCE software package. The annual reports are intended to produce a simple summary of each year's results. At least once every five years, a more substantial report will be produced after a detailed analysis of data that will look for patterns and trends in species and bird community composition, species-specific trends in abundance, and any changes in species distribution. These analyses will involve exporting data to the DISTANCE software to develop detection functions for each species and to determine the effect on various covariates such as observer, habitat, season, and weather conditions, and to apply correction factors to the data as part of the analysis for patterns and trends. For both routine annual reporting and occasional trend reporting, the database also includes a routine to export data to an excel file that can then be imported as a comma-separated-values .csv file by the R statistical package to perform additional data summaries and production of graphics for use in reports, as described in SOP #8 (Data Summary, Analysis, and Reporting). The file *CHIS_R_Scripts.R* contains code for the free statistical package R and instructions for how to run it, to streamline the analysis and graphing of data for annual reporting and for occasional trend reporting. The R code reads a data file exported from the data base and includes routines for summarizing the abundance and percent occurrence of each species during each survey (Tour), routines for producing graphics that can be used in annual reports and trend reports, as well as routines for producing histograms and boxplots of bird detection distances that will facilitate the analysis and modeling of bird detection data and the effect of different covariates on detection probabilities using DISTANCE.

5. Personnel Requirements and Training

5.1 Roles and Responsibilities

The Project Manager, who will implement this protocol and serve as one of the primary observers in the field, must be well-versed in all aspects of the protocol. The Project Manager is responsible for hiring and training field assistants; overseeing data collection, data entry, and quality control procedures; conducting routine data summaries; and preparing annual reports and occasional trend reports. Data entry will be conducted by the Project Manager and field assistants during the field season.

The responsibility for long-term data management will be shared by the Project Manager and the MEDN network Data Manager. The Project Manager is responsible for routinely reviewing field data sheets and data entry during the field season, and at the end of the field season, for thoroughly reviewing all data entered, conducting the summary analyses, and certifying the data set. The Project Manager will then provide the certified data and the appropriate metadata and tour summaries to the network Data Manager, who will be responsible for archiving the data and uploading the dataset and metadata to IRMA (Integrated Resource Management Applications) data system.

5.2 Qualifications and Training

The most essential component for the collection of credible, high-quality bird data is well-trained and experienced observers. This cannot be overemphasized. Various studies have shown that observer bias is one of the most noteworthy bias factors in trend analysis of landbird populations (Kepler and Scott 1981, Barker and Sauer 1995). Training should ensure that all observers are able to identify, by sight and sound, all of the bird species expected to be encountered in the parks and >90% of bird species that have reasonable potential to occur in the area. It is also essential that observers are able to accurately and consistently estimate distances to birds and follow standard operating procedures to ensure data quality across time. In point-transect counts, most birds are recorded aurally. Therefore, it is important to hire observers with good hearing ability to ensure consistent data collection (Ramsey and Scott 1981). The analysis of distance-sampling and occupancy data can account for differences in observer skill by using Observer as a covariate, but the ability to model these differences has limitations. Observers must be prepared both mentally and physically for the extreme weather conditions and difficult terrain of Channel Islands National Park. To ensure rigor and consistency in data collection, we will hire only qualified observers (see SOP #2). We will then train them at the beginning of each field season and will periodically test each observer's ability to identify and estimate distances to birds.

6. Operational Requirements

6.1 Annual Workload and Field Schedule

Breeding bird surveys will be conducted during the period that coincides with the peak-breeding activity of most birds (March through June, starting in March for the southern islands; see Table 1). Specific survey dates may vary slightly because of weather, road conditions, and other island conditions. The sampling window will be documented in a tour summary for each event group before leaving the island with metadata notes on unusual events. Sampling dates should be scheduled, and sampling logistics organized prior to the start of each field season.

Santa Barbara and East Anacapa Islands can be sampled in one tour by one observer. San Miguel Island can usually be sampled by two observers in one tour depending on fog and wind conditions. Santa Rosa Island sampling requires two observers for up to six tours, depending on weather and road conditions.

6.2 Procedures for Revising the Protocol

It is expected that revisions to both the Protocol Narrative and to specific Standard Operating Procedures will be necessary from time to time. Careful documentation of changes to the protocol and a library of previous protocol versions are essential for maintaining consistency in data collection and for appropriate treatment of the data during data summary and analysis.

Standard Operating Procedure #12 outlines the steps for changing either the Protocol Narrative or the SOPs. Each SOP contains a SOP Revision History Log that explains the changes and assigns a new version number to the revised SOP. The new version of the SOP and/or Protocol Narrative is then archived in the Protocol Library. The rationale for dividing a sampling protocol into a Protocol Narrative with supporting SOPs is based on the following:

- The Protocol Narrative is a general overview of the protocol that gives the history and justification for doing the work and an overview of the sampling methods, but it does not provide all of the procedural details. The Protocol Narrative will only be revised if major changes are made to the protocol.

- The SOPs are specific step-by-step instructions for performing a given task. They are expected to be revised more frequently than the Protocol Narrative. In most cases, when a SOP is revised, it is not necessary to revise the Protocol Narrative to reflect the specific changes made to the SOP.

- All versions of the Protocol Narrative and SOPs will be archived in a Protocol Library, and the event record in the database will indicate which version of the protocol was used at the time that the data were collected.

7. Literature Cited

Barker, R. J., and J. R. Sauer. 1995. Statistical aspects of point count sampling. Pages 125-130 *in* C. J. Ralph, J. R. Sauer, and S. Droege, eds. Monitoring Bird Populations by Point Counts, USDA Forest Service, Pacific Southwest Research Station, General Technical Report PSW-GTR-149.

Bibby, C. J, N. D. Burgess, D. A. Hill, and S. Mustoe. 2000. Bird census techniques. Second ed. London: Academic Press.

Bryce, S. A., R. M. Hughes, and P. R. Kaufmann. 2002. Development of a bird integrity index: Using bird assemblages as indicators of riparian condition. Environmental Management 30:294–310.

Buckland, S. T., D. R. Anderson, K. P. Burnham, J. L. Laake, D. L. Borchers, and L. Thomas. 2001. Introduction to distance sampling: Estimating abundance of biological populations. Oxford, U.K.: Oxford University Press.

Buckland, S. T., D. R. Anderson, K. P. Burnham, J. L. Laake, D. L. Borchers, and L. Thomas. 2004. Advanced distance sampling: Estimating abundance of biological populations. Oxford University Press, Oxford.

Canterbury, G. E., T. E. Martin, D. R. Petit, L. J. Petit, and D. F. Bradford. 2000. Bird communities and habitat as ecological indicators of forest condition in regional monitoring. Conservation Biology 14:544–558.

Carpenter, S. R. 1998. The need for large-scale experiments to assess and predict the response of ecosystems to perturbation. Pages 287-312 *in* M. L. Pace and P. M. Groffman, editors. Successes, limitations and frontiers in ecosystem science. Springer, New York, New York.

Coonan, T. J., G. Austin, G., and L. C. Dye. 2001. Landbird Monitoring Channel Islands National Park 1995-2000 Annual Report, Technical Report 2001-03, Channel Islands National Park. National Park Service, Ventura, California.

Coonan, T. J., L. C. Dye, and S. G. Fancy. 2011. Landbird monitoring 2011 annual report, Channel Islands National Park. Natural Resource Data Series NPS/MEDN/NRDS— 2011/214. National Park Service, Fort Collins, Colorado.

Davis, G. E. 1989. Design of a long-term ecological monitoring program for Channel Islands National Park, California. Natural Areas Journal 9:80–89.

Davis, G. E., and W. L. Halvorson. 1988. Inventory and monitoring of natural resources in Channel Islands National Park. National Park Service, Ventura, California.

Diefenbach, D. R., D. W. Brauning, and J. A. Mattice. 2003. Variability in grassland bird counts related to observer differences and species detection rates. Auk 120:1168–1179.

Diamond, J. M. 1969. Avifaunal equilibria and species turnover rates on the Channel Islands of California. Proceedings of the National Academy of Sciences 64:57–73.

Diamond, J. M.,, and H. L. Jones. 1980. Breeding land birds of the Channel Islands. Pp. 597–612 *in* D. M. Power, ed., The California Islands: Proceedings of a Multidisciplinary Symposium. Santa Barbara Museum of Natural History, Santa Barbara, California.

Fancy, S. G., J. E. Gross, and S. L. Carter. 2009. Monitoring the condition of natural resources in US national parks. Environmental Monitoring and Assessment 151:161-174.

Gostomski, T., M. Knutson, N. P. Danz, B. Route, and T. W. Sutherland. 2010. Landbird monitoring protocol, Great Lakes Inventory and Monitoring Network. Natural Resource Report NPS/GLKN/NRR – 2010/225. National Park Service, Fort Collins, Colorado.

Halvorson, W. L., S. D. Veirs, Jr., R. A. Clark, and D. D. Borgais. 1988. Terrestrial vegetation monitoring handbook, Channel Islands National Park, California. National Park Service, Ventura, California.

Johnson, N. K. 1972. Origin and differentiation of the avifauna of the Channel Islands, California. Condor 74:295–315.

Kepler, C. B., and J. M. Scott. 1981. Reducing bird count variability by training observers. Studies in Avian Biology 6:366–371.

Lovett, G. M., D. A. Burns, C. T. Driscoll, J. C. Jenkins, M. J. Mitchell, L. Rustad, J. B. Shanley, G. E Likens, and R. Haeuber. 2007. Who needs environmental monitoring? Frontiers in Ecology and the Environment 5:253–260.

Lynch, J. F., and N. K. Johnson. 1974. Turnover and equilibria in insular avifaunas, with special reference to the California Channel Islands. Condor 76:370–384.

McEachern, Kathryn. 2000. Channel Islands National Park Landbird Monitoring Program Review, April 18–19, 2000. USGS Open File Report, 9 pp.

National Park Service. 2006. Management policies 2006. http://www.nps.gov/policy/MP2006.pdf (accessed 14 December 2011).

Nelson, J. T., and S. G. Fancy. 1999. A test of the variable circular-plot method where exact density of a bird population was known. Pacific Conservation Biology 5:139–143.

Oakley, K. L., L. P. Thomas, and S. G. Fancy. 2003. Guidelines for long-term monitoring protocols. Wildlife Society Bulletin 31:1000-1003.

Peitz, D. G., S. G. Fancy, L. P. Thomas, G. A. Rowell, and M. D. Debacker. 2004. Bird monitoring protocol for Agate Fossil Beds National Monument, Nebraska and Tallgrass Prairie National Preserve, Kansas. Prairie Cluster Prototype Long-term Ecological Monitoring Program, National Park Service, Department of the Interior.

Powell, B. F., A. D. Flesch, D. Angell, K. Beaupre, and W. L. Halvorson. 2007. Landbird monitoring protocol for the Sonoran Desert Network. Version 1.02. Natural Resource Report NPS/SODN/NRR-2007/021. National Park Service, Fort Collins, Colorado.

Ralph, C. J., J. R. Sauer, and S. Droege (editors). 1995. Monitoring bird populations by point counts. General Technical Report PSW-GTR-149. Pacific Southwest Research Station, Forest Service, U.S. Department of Agriculture. Albany, California.

Ramsey, F. L. and J. M. Scott. 1981. Tests of hearing ability. Studies in Avian Biology 6:341-345.

Reynolds, R. T., J. M. Scott, and R. N. Nussbaum. 1980. A variable circular-plot method for estimating bird numbers. Condor 82:309–313.

Rosenstock, S. S., D. R. Anderson, K. M. Giesen, T. Leukering, and M. F. Carter. 2002. Landbird counting techniques: Current practices and an alternative. Auk 119:46–53.

Royle, J. A., and W. A. Link. 2006. Generalized site occupancy models allowing for false positive and false negative errors. Ecology 87:835–841.

Sekercioglu, C. H. 2002. Impacts of birdwatching on human and avian communities. Environmental Conservation 29:282–289.

Siegel, R. B., R. L. Wilkerson, K. J. Jenkins, R. C. Kuntz II, J. R. Boetsch, J. P. Schaberl, and P. J. Happe. 2007. Landbird Monitoring Protocol for National Parks in the North Coast and Cascades Network. U.S. Geological Survey Techniques and Methods 2-A6. 208 pp.

Siegel, R. B., R. L. Wilkerson, and M. Goldin Rose. 2010. Bird monitoring protocol for national parks in the Sierra Nevada Network. Natural Resource Report NPS/SIEN/NRR—2010/231. National Park Service, Fort Collins, Colorado.

Simons, T. R., K. H. Pollack, J. M. Wettroth, M. W. Alldredge, K. Pacifici, and J. Brewster. 2009. Sources of measurement error, misclassification error, and bias in auditory avian point count data. Pages 237–254 in D. L. Thomson et al., editors. Modeling demographic processes in marked populations. Environmental and ecological statistics Volume 3. Springer Science+Business Media, LLC. DOI 10.1007/978-0-387-78151-8_10.

Sogge, M. K., C. van Riper III, and C. Drost. 1989. Design considerations for monitoring land birds in Channel Islands National Park. 1989 Transactions of the Western Section of the Wildlife Society 25: 65–71.

Stephens, J. L., S. R. Mohren, J. D. Alexander, D. A. Sarr, and K. M. Irvine. 2010. Klamath Network landbird monitoring protocol. Natural Resource Report NPS/KLMN/NRR—2010/187. National Park Service, Fort Collins, Colorado.

Super, P. E., C. van Riper III, and M. K. Sogge. 1991. Santa Rosa Island land bird monitoring handbook. Channel Islands National Park, California. National Park Service, Ventura, California.

van Riper, C., III, M. K. Sogge, and C. Drost. 1988. Land bird monitoring handbook, Channel Islands National Park, California. National Park Service, Ventura, California.

Appendix A. Master Bird List for Channel Islands National Park (as of December 2011).

Order	Family	Scientific Name	Common Name	Symbol	Abundance	Residency	Nativity	TSN
Anseriformes	Anatidae	Aix sponsa	Wood Duck	WODU	Occasional	Vagrant	Native	175122
Anseriformes	Anatidae	Anas acuta	Northern Pintail	NOPI	Occasional	Migratory	Native	175074
Anseriformes	Anatidae	Anas americana	American Wigeon	AMWI	Common	Migratory	Native	175094
Anseriformes	Anatidae	Anas clypeata	Northern Shoveler	NSHO	Occasional	Vagrant	Native	175096
Anseriformes	Anatidae	Anas crecca	Green-winged Teal	GWTE	Common	Migratory	Native	175081
Anseriformes	Anatidae	Anas cyanoptera	Cinnamon Teal	CITE	Uncommon	Migratory	Native	175089
Anseriformes	Anatidae	Anas discors	Blue-winged Teal	BWTE	Rare	Vagrant	Native	175086
Anseriformes	Anatidae	Anas penelope	Eurasian Wigeon	EUWI	Occasional	Vagrant	Native	175092
Anseriformes	Anatidae	Anasv platyrhynchos	Mallard	MALL	Rare	Breeder	Native	175063
Anseriformes	Anatidae	Anser albifrons	Greater White-fronted Goose	GWFG	Rare	Vagrant	Native	175020
Anseriformes	Anatidae	Aythya affins	Lesser Scaup	LESC	Occasional	Vagrant	Native	175134
Anseriformes	Anatidae	Aythya americana	Redhead	REDH	Occasional	Vagrant	Native	175125
Anseriformes	Anatidae	Aythya collaris	Ring-necked Duck	RNDU	Occasional	Vagrant	Native	175128
Anseriformes	Anatidae	Aythya valisineria	Canvasback	CANV	Occasional	Vagrant	Native	175129
Anseriformes	Anatidae	Branta bernicla	Brant	BRAN	Rare	Migratory	Native	175011
Anseriformes	Anatidae	Branta canadensis	Canada Goose	CANG	Rare	Migratory	Native	174999
Anseriformes	Anatidae	Bucephala albeola	Bufflehead	BUFF	Occasional	Vagrant	Native	175145
Anseriformes	Anatidae	Bucephala clangula	Common Goldeneye	COGO	Occasional	Vagrant	Native	175141
Anseriformes	Anatidae	Chen caerulescens	Snow Goose	SNGO	Rare	Migratory	Native	175038
Anseriformes	Anatidae	Chen rossii	Ross' Goose	ROGO	Occasional	Vagrant	Native	175041
Anseriformes	Anatidae	Histrionicus histrionicus	Harlequin Duck	HADU	Occasional	Vagrant	Native	175149
Anseriformes	Anatidae	Lophodytes cucullatus	Hooded Merganser	HOME	Occasional	Vagrant	Native	175183
Anseriformes	Anatidae	Melanitta fusca	White-winged Scoter	WWSC	Common	Migratory	Native	175163
Anseriformes	Anatidae	Melanitta nigra	Black Scoter	BLSC	Occasional	Vagrant	Native	175171
Anseriformes	Anatidae	Melanitta perspicillata	Surf Scoter	SUSC	Abundant	Migratory	Native	175170
Anseriformes	Anatidae	Mergus serrator	Red-breasted Merganser	RBME	Uncommon	Migratory	Native	175187
Anseriformes	Anatidae	Oxyura jamaicensis	Ruddy Duck	RUDU	Rare	Migratory	Native	175175
Apodiformes	Apodidae	Aeronautes saxatalis	White-throated Swift	WTSW	Uncommon	Breeder	Native	178014
Apodiformes	Apodidae	Chaetura pelagica	Chimney Swift	CHSW	Occasional	Vagrant	Native	178001
Apodiformes	Apodidae	Chaetura vauxi	Vaux's Swift	VASW	Uncommon	Vagrant	Native	178002

Order	Family	Scientific Name	Common Name	Code	Abundance	Occurrence	Origin	TSN
Apodiformes	Apodidae	Cypseloides niger	Black Swift	BLSW	Occasional	Vagrant	Native	177997
Apodiformes	Trochilidae	Archilochus alerandri	Black-chinned Hummingbird	BCHU	Occasional	Vagrant	Native	178033
Apodiformes	Trochilidae	Calypte anna	Anna's Hummingbird	ANHU	Uncommon	Breeder	Native	178036
Apodiformes	Trochilidae	Calypte costae	Costa's Hummingbird	COHU	Rare	Breeder	Native	178035
Apodiformes	Trochilidae	Selasphorus rufus	Rufous Hummingbird	RUHU	Uncommon	Vagrant	Native	178040
Apodiformes	Trochilidae	Selasphorus sasin	Allen's Hummingbird	ALHU	Abundant	Breeder	Native	178041
Apodiformes	Trochilidae	Stellula calliope	Calliope Hummingbird	CAHU	Occasional	Vagrant	Native	178048
Ciconiiformes	Accipitridae	Accipiter cooperii	Cooper's Hawk	COHA	Occasional	Breeder	Native	175309
Ciconiiformes	Accipitridae	Accipiter gentilis	Northern Goshawk	NOGO	Occasional	Vagrant	Native	175300
Ciconiiformes	Accipitridae	Accipiter striatus	Sharp-shinned Hawk	SSHA	Uncommon	Migratory	Native	175304
Ciconiiformes	Accipitridae	Aquila chrysaetos	Golden Eagle	GOEA	Rare	Breeder	Native	175407
Ciconiiformes	Accipitridae	Buteo jamaicensis	Red-tailed Hawk	RTHA	Common	Breeder	Native	175350
Ciconiiformes	Accipitridae	Buteo lagopus	Rough-legged Hawk	RLHA	Occasional	Vagrant	Native	175373
Ciconiiformes	Accipitridae	Buteo swainsoni	Swainson's Hawk	SWHA	Occasional	Vagrant	Native	175367
Ciconiiformes	Accipitridae	Circus cyaneus	Northern Harrier	NOHA	Rare	Migratory	Native	175430
Ciconiiformes	Accipitridae	Elanus leucurus	White-tailed Kite	WTKI	Occasional	Vagrant	Native	175282
Ciconiiformes	Accipitridae	Haliaeetus leucocephalus	Bald Eagle	BAEA	Uncommon	Breeder	Native	175420
Ciconiiformes	Accipitridae	Pandion haliaetus	Osprey	OSPR	Occasional	Migratory	Native	175590
Ciconiiformes	Alcidae	Brachyramphus marmoratus	Marbled Murrelet	MAMU	Occasional	Vagrant	Native	176996
Ciconiiformes	Alcidae	Cepphus columba	Pigeon Guillemot	PIGU	Uncommon	Breeder	Native	176991
Ciconiiformes	Alcidae	Cerorhinca monocerata	Rhinoceros Auklet	RHAU	Occasional	Breeder	Native	177023
Ciconiiformes	Alcidae	Fratercula cirrhata	Tufted Puffin	TUPU	Occasional	Breeder	Native	177032
Ciconiiformes	Alcidae	Fratercula corniculata	Horned Puffin	HOPU	Occasional	Vagrant	Native	177029
Ciconiiformes	Alcidae	Ptychoramphus aleuticus	Cassin's Auklet	CAAU	Common	Breeder	Native	177013
Ciconiiformes	Alcidae	Synthliboramphus antiquus	Ancient Murrelet	ANMU	Occasional	Vagrant	Native	177008
Ciconiiformes	Alcidae	Synthliboramphus craveri	Craveri's Murrelet	CRMU	Occasional	Vagrant	Native	177010
Ciconiiformes	Alcidae	Synthliboramphus hypoleucus	Xantus' Murrelet	XAMU	Common	Breeder	Native	177011
Ciconiiformes	Alcidae	Uria aalge	Common Murre	COMU	Uncommon	Migratory	Native	176974
Ciconiiformes	Ardeidae	Ardea alba	Great Egret	GREG	Occasional	Vagrant	Native	554135
Ciconiiformes	Ardeidae	Ardea herodias	Great Blue Heron	GBHE	Uncommon	Migratory	Native	174773
Ciconiiformes	Ardeidae	Bubulcus ibis	Cattle Egret	CAEG	Rare	Migratory	Native	174803
Ciconiiformes	Ardeidae	Butorides virescens	Green Heron	GRHE	Rare	Vagrant	Native	174793
Ciconiiformes	Ardeidae	Egretta thula	Snowy Egret	SNEG	Occasional	Vagrant	Native	174813
Ciconiiformes	Ardeidae	Nycticorax nycticorax	Black-crowned Night-Heron	BCNH	Occasional	Migratory	Native	174832

Ciconiiformes	Charadriidae	Charadrius alexandrinus	Snowy Plover	SNPL	Rare	Breeder	Native	176510
Ciconiiformes	Charadriidae	Charadrius montanus	Mountain Plover	MOPL	Rare	Migratory	Native	176522
Ciconiiformes	Charadriidae	Charadrius semipalmatus	Semipalmated Plover	SEPL	Rare	Vagrant	Native	176506
Ciconiiformes	Charadriidae	Charadrius vociferus	Killdeer	KILL	Rare	Vagrant	Native	176520
Ciconiiformes	Charadriidae	Haematopus bachmani	Black Oystercatcher	BLOY	Rare	Breeder	Native	176475
Ciconiiformes	Charadriidae	Haematopus palliatus	American Oystercatcher	AMOY	Occasional	Breeder	Native	176472
Ciconiiformes	Charadriidae	Himantopus mexicanus	Black-necked Stilt	BNST	Occasional	Vagrant	Native	176726
Ciconiiformes	Charadriidae	Pluvialis dominica	Lesser Golden-Plover	AMGP	Rare	Migratory	Native	176564
Ciconiiformes	Charadriidae	Pluvialis squatarola	Black-bellied Plover	BBPL	Abundant	Migratory	Native	176567
Ciconiiformes	Charadriidae	Recurvirostra americana	American Avocet	AMAV	Occasional	Vagrant	Native	176721
Ciconiiformes	Diomedeidae	Diomedea albatrus	Short-tailed Albatross	STAL	Occasional	Vagrant	Native	174515
Ciconiiformes	Diomedeidae	Diomedea immutabilis	Laysan Albatross	LAAL	Occasional	Vagrant	Native	174517
Ciconiiformes	Diomedeidae	Diomedea nigripes	Black-footed Albatross	BFAL	Occasional	Migratory	Native	174516
Ciconiiformes	Falconidae	Falco columbarius	Merlin	MERL	Rare	Migratory	Native	175613
Ciconiiformes	Falconidae	Falco mexicanus	Prairie Falcon	PRFA	Occasional	Vagrant	Native	175603
Ciconiiformes	Falconidae	Falco peregrinus	Peregrine Falcon	PEFA	Rare	Breeder	Native	175604
Ciconiiformes	Falconidae	Falco sparverius	American Kestrel	AMKE	Rare	Breeder	Native	175622
Ciconiiformes	Fregatidae	Fregata magnificens	Magnificent Frigatebird	MAFR	Occasional	Migratory	Native	174763
Ciconiiformes	Gaviidae	Gavia immer	Common Loon	COLO	Common	Vagrant	Native	174469
Ciconiiformes	Gaviidae	Gavia pacifica	Pacific Loon	PALO	Abundant	Vagrant	Native	174475
Ciconiiformes	Gaviidae	Gavia stellata	Red-throated Loon	RTLO	Uncommon	Vagrant	Native	174474
Ciconiiformes	Hydrobatidae	Oceanodroma homochroa	Ashy Storm-Petrel	ASSP	Common	Breeder	Native	174634
Ciconiiformes	Hydrobatidae	Oceanodroma leucorhoa	Leach's Storm-Petrel	LESP	Uncommon	Breeder	Native	174628
Ciconiiformes	Hydrobatidae	Oceanodroma melania	Black Storm-Petrel	BLSP	Common	Breeder	Native	174640
Ciconiiformes	Hydrobatidae	Oceanodroma microsoma	Least Storm-Petrel	LSTP	Occasional	Vagrant	Native	174646
Ciconiiformes	Laridae	Larus argentatus	Herring Gull	HERG	Uncommon	Migratory	Native	176824
Ciconiiformes	Laridae	Larus atricilla	Laughing Gull	LAGU	Occasional	Vagrant	Native	176837
Ciconiiformes	Laridae	Larus californicus	California Gull	CAGU	Common	Migratory	Native	176829
Ciconiiformes	Laridae	Larus canus	Mew Gull	MEGU	Common	Migratory	Native	176832
Ciconiiformes	Laridae	Larus delawarensis	Ring-billed Gull	RBGU	Occasional	Vagrant	Native	176830
Ciconiiformes	Laridae	Larus glaucescens	Glaucous-winged Gull	GWGU	Common	Migratory	Native	176814
Ciconiiformes	Laridae	Larus heermanni	Heermann's Gull	HEEG	Abundant	Migratory	Native	176841
Ciconiiformes	Laridae	Larus hyperboreus	Glaucous Gull	GLGU	Occasional	Vagrant	Native	176808
Ciconiiformes	Laridae	Larus occidentalis	Western Gull	WEGU	Abundant	Breeder	Native	176817

31

Order	Family	Scientific Name	Common Name	Code	Abundance	Status	Origin	Number
Ciconiiformes	Laridae	Larus philadelphia	Bonaparte's Gull	BOGU	Uncommon	Migratory	Native	176839
Ciconiiformes	Laridae	Larus pipixcan	Franklin's Gull	FRGU	Occasional	Vagrant	Native	176838
Ciconiiformes	Laridae	Larus thayeri	Thayer's Gull	THGU	Occasional	Vagrant	Native	176828
Ciconiiformes	Laridae	Rissa tridactyla	Black-legged Kittiwake	BLKI	Uncommon	Migratory	Native	176875
Ciconiiformes	Laridae	Sterna caspia	Caspian Tern	CATE	Occasional	Vagrant	Native	176924
Ciconiiformes	Laridae	Sterna elegans	Elegant Tern	ELTE	Occasional	Vagrant	Native	176925
Ciconiiformes	Laridae	Sterna forsteri	Forster's Tern	FOTE	Rare	Vagrant	Native	176887
Ciconiiformes	Laridae	Sterna maxima	Royal Tern	ROYT	Common	Migratory	Native	176922
Ciconiiformes	Laridae	Sterna paradisaea	Arctic Tern	ARTE	Occasional	Vagrant	Native	176890
Ciconiiformes	Laridae	Xema sabini	Sabine's Gull	SAGU	Occasional	Vagrant	Native	176866
Ciconiiformes	Pelecanidae	Pelecanus erythrorhynchos	American White Pelican	AWPE	Abundant	Vagrant	Native	174684
Ciconiiformes	Pelecanidae	Pelecanus occidentalis	Brown Pelican	BRPE	Abundant	Breeder	Native	174685
Ciconiiformes	Phaethontidae	Phaethon aethereus	Red-billed Tropicbird	RBTR	Occasional	Vagrant	Native	174673
Ciconiiformes	Phalacrocoracidae	Phalacrocorax auritus	Double-crested Cormorant	DCCO	Common	Breeder	Native	174717
Ciconiiformes	Phalacrocoracidae	Phalacrocorax pelagicus	Pelagic Cormorant	PECO	Common	Breeder	Native	174725
Ciconiiformes	Phalacrocoracidae	Phalacrocorax penicillatus	Brandt's Cormorant	BRAC	Abundant	Breeder	Native	174724
Ciconiiformes	Podicipedidae	Aechmophorus clarkii	Clark's Grebe	CLGR	Occasional	Vagrant	Native	554027
Ciconiiformes	Podicipedidae	Aechmophorus occidentalis	Western Grebe	WEGR	Common	Migratory	Native	174503
Ciconiiformes	Podicipedidae	Podiceps auritus	Horned Grebe	HOGR	Common	Migratory	Native	174482
Ciconiiformes	Podicipedidae	Podiceps nigricollis	Eared Grebe	EAGR	Abundant	Migratory	Native	174485
Ciconiiformes	Podicipedidae	Podilymbus podiceps	Pied-billed Grebe	PBGR	Occasional	Vagrant	Native	174505
Ciconiiformes	Procellariidae	Fulmarus glacialis	Northern Fulmar	NOFU	Uncommon	Migratory	Native	174536
Ciconiiformes	Procellariidae	Puffinus carneipes	Flesh-footed Shearwater	FFSH	Occasional	Vagrant	Native	174548
Ciconiiformes	Procellariidae	Puffinus creatopus	Pink-footed Shearwater	PFSH	Rare	Migratory	Native	174547
Ciconiiformes	Procellariidae	Puffinus griseus	Sooty Shearwater	SOSH	Uncommon	Migratory	Native	174553
Ciconiiformes	Procellariidae	Puffinus opisthomelas	Black-vented Shearwater	BVSH	Rare	Vagrant	Native	554396
Ciconiiformes	Scolopacidae	Actitis macularia	Spotted Sandpiper	SPSA	Uncommon	Migratory	Native	176612
Ciconiiformes	Scolopacidae	Aphriza virgata	Surfbird	SURF	Rare	Vagrant	Native	176673
Ciconiiformes	Scolopacidae	Arenaria interpres	Ruddy Turnstone	RUTU	Common	Vagrant	Native	176571
Ciconiiformes	Scolopacidae	Arenaria melanocephala	Black Turnstone	BLTU	Abundant	Migratory	Native	176574
Ciconiiformes	Scolopacidae	Bartramia longicauda	Upland Sandpiper	UPSA	Occasional	Vagrant	Native	176610
Ciconiiformes	Scolopacidae	Calidris alba	Sanderling	SAND	Abundant	Migratory	Native	176669
Ciconiiformes	Scolopacidae	Calidris alpina	Dunlin	DUNL	Uncommon	Migratory	Native	176661
Ciconiiformes	Scolopacidae	Calidris bairdii	Baird's Sandpiper	BASA	Occasional	Vagrant	Native	176655

Order	Family	Scientific name	Common name	Code	Abundance	Status	Native	ID
Ciconiiformes	Scolopacidae	Calidris canutus	Red Knot	REKN	Occasional	Vagrant	Native	176642
Ciconiiformes	Scolopacidae	Calidris mauri	Western Sandpiper	WESA	Uncommon	Vagrant	Native	176668
Ciconiiformes	Scolopacidae	Calidris melanotos	Pectoral Sandpiper	PESA	Rare	Vagrant	Native	176653
Ciconiiformes	Scolopacidae	Calidris minutilla	Least Sandpiper	LESA	Common	Unknown	Native	176656
Ciconiiformes	Scolopacidae	Catoptrophorus semipalmatus	Willet	WILL	Abundant	Migratory	Native	176638
Ciconiiformes	Scolopacidae	Gallinago gallinago	Common Snipe	COSN	Uncommon	Vagrant	Native	176700
Ciconiiformes	Scolopacidae	Heteroscelus incanus	Wandering Tattler	WATA	Common	Migratory	Native	176635
Ciconiiformes	Scolopacidae	Limnodromus griseus	Short-billed Dowitcher	SBDO	Occasional	Vagrant	Native	176675
Ciconiiformes	Scolopacidae	Limnodromus scolopaceus	Long-billed Dowitcher	LBDO	Rare	Vagrant	Native	176679
Ciconiiformes	Scolopacidae	Limosa fedoa	Marbled Godwit	MAGO	Abundant	Migratory	Native	176686
Ciconiiformes	Scolopacidae	Numenius americanus	Long-billed Curlew	LBCU	Uncommon	Migratory	Native	176593
Ciconiiformes	Scolopacidae	Numenius phaeopus	Whimbrel	WHIM	Common	Migratory	Native	176599
Ciconiiformes	Scolopacidae	Phalaropus fulicaria	Red Phalarope	REPH	Rare	Migratory	Native	554376
Ciconiiformes	Scolopacidae	Phalaropus lobatus	Red-necked Phalarope	RNPH	Rare	Vagrant	Native	176735
Ciconiiformes	Scolopacidae	Phalaropus tricolor	Wilson's Phalarope	WIPH	Occasional	Vagrant	Native	176736
Ciconiiformes	Scolopacidae	Tringa flavipes	Lesser Yellowlegs	LEYE	Occasional	Vagrant	Native	176620
Ciconiiformes	Scolopacidae	Tringa melanoleuca	Greater Yellowlegs	GRYE	Rare	Vagrant	Native	176619
Ciconiiformes	Scolopacidae	Tringa solitaria	Solitary Sandpiper	SOSA	Rare	Vagrant	Native	176615
Ciconiiformes	Scolopacidae	Tryngites subruficollis	Buff-breasted Sandpiper	BBSA	Occasional	Vagrant	Native	176684
Ciconiiformes	Stercorariidae	Stercorarius longicaudus	Long-tailed Jaeger	LTJA	Occasional	Vagrant	Native	176794
Ciconiiformes	Stercorariidae	Stercorarius maccormicki	South Polar Skua	SPSK	Occasional	Vagrant	Native	660062
Ciconiiformes	Stercorariidae	Stercorarius parasiticus	Parasitic Jaeger	PAJA	Rare	Migratory	Native	176793
Ciconiiformes	Stercorariidae	Stercorarius pomarinus	Pomarine Jaeger	POJA	Occasional	Vagrant	Native	176792
Ciconiiformes	Sulidae	Sula leucogaster	Brown Booby	BRBO	Occasional	Vagrant	Native	174704
Ciconiiformes	Sulidae	Sula nebouxii	Blue-footed Booby	BFBO	Occasional	Vagrant	Native	174702
Ciconiiformes	Sulidae	Sula sula	Red-footed Booby	RFBO	Occasional	Vagrant	Native	174707
Columbiformes	Columbidae	Columba fasciata	Band-tailed Pigeon	BTPI	Uncommon	Migratory	Native	177065
Columbiformes	Columbidae	Columba livia	Rock Dove	ROPI	Rare	Breeder	Native	177071
Columbiformes	Columbidae	Streptopelia chinensis	Spotted Dove	SPDO	Occasional	Vagrant	Native	177134
Columbiformes	Columbidae	Streptopelia risoria	Ringed Turtle-Dove	RITD	Occasional	Vagrant	Native	177136
Columbiformes	Columbidae	Zenaida asiatica	White-winged Dove	WWDO	Occasional	Vagrant	Native	177121
Columbiformes	Columbidae	Zenaida macroura	Mourning Dove	MODO	Uncommon	Breeder	Native	177125
Coraciiformes	Alcedinidae	Ceryle alcyon	Belted Kingfisher	BEKI	Uncommon	Migratory	Native	178119
Cuculiformes	Cuculidae	Coccyzus americanus	Yellow-billed Cuckoo	YBCU	Occasional	Vagrant	Native	177831

TSN	Origin	Occurrence	Abundance	Code	Common Name	Scientific Name	Family	Order
177834	Native	Vagrant	Occasional	BBCU	Black-billed Cuckoo	Coccyzus erythropthalmus	Cuculidae	Cuculiformes
175876	Non-Native	Breeder	Common	CAQU	California Quail	Callipepla californica	Odontophoridae	Galliformes
175877	Non-Native	NA	NA	GAQU	Gambel's Quail	Callipepla gambelii	Odontophoridae	Galliformes
175908	Non-Native	NA	NA	CHUK	Chukar	Alectoris chukar	Phasianidae	Galliformes
176136	Non-Native	Breeder	Rare	WITU	Wild Turkey	Meleagris gallopavo	Phasianidae	Galliformes
176113	Non-Native	Breeder	Rare	CPEA	Common Peafowl	Pavo cristatus	Phasianidae	Galliformes
175905	Non-Native	Vagrant	Occasional	RNPH	Ring-necked Pheasent	Phasianus	Phasianidae	Galliformes
176292	Native	Breeder	Occasional	AMCO	American Coot	Fulica americana	Rallidae	Gruiformes
176242	Native	Vagrant	Rare	SORA	Sora	Porzana carolina	Rallidae	Gruiformes
176221	Native	Breeder	Occasional	VIRA	Virginia Rail	Rallus limicola	Rallidae	Gruiformes
178764	Native	Breeder	Common	BUSH	Bushtit	Psaltriparus minimus	Aegithalidae	Passeriformes
554256	Native	Breeder	Abundant	HOLA	Horned Lark	Eremophila alpestris	Alaudidae	Passeriformes
178532	Native	Vagrant	Uncommon	CEDW	Cedar Waxwing	Bombycilla cedrorum	Bombycillidae	Passeriformes
179132	Native	Vagrant	Occasional	PYRR	Pyrrhuloxia	Cardinalis sinuatus	Cardinalidae	Passeriformes
179145	Native	Vagrant	Rare	BLGR	Blue Grosbeak	Guiraca caerulea	Cardinalidae	Passeriformes
179151	Native	Breeder	Occasional	LAZB	Lazuli Bunting	Passerina amoena	Cardinalidae	Passeriformes
179150	Native	Vagrant	Uncommon	INBU	Indigo Bunting	Passerina cyanea	Cardinalidae	Passeriformes
179139	Native	Vagrant	Uncommon	RBGR	Rose-breasted Grosbeak	Pheucticus ludovicianus	Cardinalidae	Passeriformes
179140	Native	Breeder	Rare	BHGR	Black-headed Grosbeak	Pheucticus melanocephalus	Cardinalidae	Passeriformes
179165	Native	Vagrant	Occasional	DICK	Dickcissel	Spiza americana	Cardinalidae	Passeriformes
178803	Native	Migratory	Rare	BRCR	Brown Creeper	Certhia americana	Certhiidae	Passeriformes
179853	Native	Breeder	Uncommon	BGGN	Blue-gray Gnatcatcher	Polioptila caerulea	Certhiidae	Passeriformes
178536	Native	Vagrant	Occasional	AMDI	American Dipper	Cinclus mexicanus	Cinclidae	Passeriformes
554129	Native	Breeder	Common	ISSJ	Island Scrub Jay	Aphelocoma insularis	Corvidae	Passeriformes
179731	Native	Vagrant	Occasional	AMCR	American Crow	Corvus brachyrhynchos	Corvidae	Passeriformes
179725	Native	Breeder	Uncommon	CORA	Common Raven	Corvus corax	Corvidae	Passeriformes
179750	Native	Migratory	Occasional	CLNU	Clark's Nutcracker	Nucifraga columbiana	Corvidae	Passeriformes
179723	Native	Vagrant	Occasional	YBMA	Yellow-billed Magpie	Pica nuttalli	Corvidae	Passeriformes
179377	Native	Breeder	Uncommon	RCSP	Rufous-crowned Sparrow	Aimophila ruficeps	Emberizidae	Passeriformes
179333	Native	Breeder	Rare	GRSP	Grasshopper Sparrow	Ammodramus savannarum	Emberizidae	Passeriformes
179402	Native	Vagrant	Occasional	SAGS	Sage Sparrow	Amphispiza belli	Emberizidae	Passeriformes
179395	Native	Vagrant	Rare	BTSP	Black-throated Sparrow	Amphispiza bilineata	Emberizidae	Passeriformes
179312	Native	Vagrant	Occasional	LARB	Lark Bunting	Calamospiza melanocorys	Emberizidae	Passeriformes
179526	Native	Vagrant	Occasional	LALO	Lapland Longspur	Calcarius lapponicus	Emberizidae	Passeriformes

Order	Family	Scientific name	Common name	Code	Abundance	Status	Origin	Number
Passeriformes	Emberizidae	Calcarius mccownii	McCown's Longspur	MCLO	Occasional	Vagrant	Native	179525
Passeriformes	Emberizidae	Calcarius ornatus	Chestnut-collared Longspur	CCLO	Occasional	Vagrant	Native	179530
Passeriformes	Emberizidae	Chondestes grammacus	Lark Sparrow	LASP	Common	Vagrant	Native	179371
Passeriformes	Emberizidae	Junco hyemalis	Dark-eyed Junco	DEJU	Common	Migratory	Native	179410
Passeriformes	Emberizidae	Melospiza georgiana	Swamp Sparrow	SWSP	Occasional	Vagrant	Native	179488
Passeriformes	Emberizidae	Melospiza lincolnii	Lincoln's Sparrow	LISP	Uncommon	Migratory	Native	179484
Passeriformes	Emberizidae	Melospiza melodia	Song Sparrow	SOSP	Common	Breeder	Native	179492
Passeriformes	Emberizidae	Passerculus sandwichensis	Savannah Sparrow	SAVS	Common	Migratory	Native	179314
Passeriformes	Emberizidae	Passerella iliaca	Fox Sparrow	FOSP	Common	Migratory	Native	179464
Passeriformes	Emberizidae	Pipilo chlorurus	Green-tailed Towhee	GTTO	Rare	Vagrant	Native	179310
Passeriformes	Emberizidae	Pipilo maculatus	Spotted Towhee	SPTO	Uncommon	Breeder	Native	554380
Passeriformes	Emberizidae	Pooecetes gramineus	Vesper Sparrow	VESP	Uncommon	Vagrant	Native	179366
Passeriformes	Emberizidae	Spizella arborea	American Tree Sparrow	ATSP	Occasional	Vagrant	Native	179432
Passeriformes	Emberizidae	Spizella atrogularis	Black-chinned Sparrow	BCSP	Occasional	Vagrant	Native	179448
Passeriformes	Emberizidae	Spizella breweri	Brewer's Sparrow	BRSP	Occasional	Vagrant	Native	179440
Passeriformes	Emberizidae	Spizella pallida	Clay-colored Sparrow	CCSP	Rare	Vagrant	Native	179439
Passeriformes	Emberizidae	Spizella passerina	Chipping Sparrow	CHSP	Common	Breeder	Native	179435
Passeriformes	Emberizidae	Zonotrichia albicollis	White-throated Sparrow	WTSP	Occasional	Vagrant	Native	179462
Passeriformes	Emberizidae	Zonotrichia atricapilla	Golden-crowned Sparrow	GCSP	Abundant	Migratory	Native	179461
Passeriformes	Emberizidae	Zonotrichia leucophrys	White-crowned Sparrow	WCSP	Abundant	Migratory	Native	179455
Passeriformes	Emberizidae	Zonotrichia querula	Harris' Sparrow	HASP	Occasional	Vagrant	Native	179454
Passeriformes	Emberizidae	Carduelis lawrencei	Lawrence's Goldfinch	LAGO	Rare	Vagrant	Native	179232
Passeriformes	Fringillidae	Carduelis pinus	Pine Siskin	PISI	Uncommon	Vagrant	Native	179233
Passeriformes	Fringillidae	Carduelis psaltria	Lesser Goldfinch	LEGO	Uncommon	Breeder	Native	179234
Passeriformes	Fringillidae	Carduelis tristis	American Goldfinch	AMGO	Rare	Migratory	Native	179236
Passeriformes	Fringillidae	Carpodacus mexicanus	House Finch	HOFI	Common	Breeder	Native	179191
Passeriformes	Fringillidae	Carpodacus purpureus	Purple Finch	PUFI	Uncommon	Migratory	Native	179186
Passeriformes	Fringillidae	Loxia curvirostra	Red Crossbill	RECR	Rare	Migratory	Native	179259
Passeriformes	Hirundinidae	Hirundo rustica	Barn Swallow	BARS	Uncommon	Breeder	Native	178448
Passeriformes	Hirundinidae	Petrochelidon pyrrhonota	Cliff Swallow	CLSW	Occasional	Breeder	Native	178455
Passeriformes	Hirundinidae	Progne subis	Purple Martin	PUMA	Occasional	Vagrant	Native	178464
Passeriformes	Hirundinidae	Riparia riparia	Bank Swallow	BANS	Occasional	Vagrant	Native	178436
Passeriformes	Hirundinidae	Stelgidopteryx serripennis	Northern Rough-winged Swallow	NRWS	Rare	Vagrant	Native	178443

Order	Family	Scientific Name	Common Name	Code	Abundance	Status	Origin	TSN
Passeriformes	Hirundinidae	Tachycineta bicolor	Tree Swallow	TRES	Rare	Vagrant	Native	178431
Passeriformes	Hirundinidae	Tachycineta thalassina	Violet-green Swallow	VGSW	Rare	Vagrant	Native	178427
Passeriformes	Icteridae	Agelaius phoeniceus	Red-winged Blackbird	RWBL	Uncommon	Breeder	Native	179045
Passeriformes	Icteridae	Agelaius tricolor	Tricolored Blackbird	TRBL	Rare	Vagrant	Native	179060
Passeriformes	Icteridae	Dolichonyx oryzivorus	Bobolink	BOBO	Rare	Vagrant	Native	179032
Passeriformes	Icteridae	Euphagus carolinus	Rusty Blackbird	RUBL	Occasional	Vagrant	Native	179091
Passeriformes	Icteridae	Euphagus cyanocephalus	Brewer's Blackbird	BRBL	Rare	Breeder	Native	179094
Passeriformes	Icteridae	Icterus bullockii	Bullock's Oriole	BUOR	Uncommon	Vagrant	Native	554267
Passeriformes	Icteridae	Icterus cucullatus	Hooded Oriole	HOOR	Rare	Vagrant	Native	179070
Passeriformes	Icteridae	Icterus galbula	Baltimore Oriole	BAOR	Uncommon	Vagrant	Native	179083
Passeriformes	Icteridae	Icterus parisorum	Scott's Oriole	SCOR	Occasional	Vagrant	Native	179082
Passeriformes	Icteridae	Molothrus ater	Brown-headed Cowbird	BHCO	Uncommon	Migratory	Native	179112
Passeriformes	Icteridae	Sturnella neglecta	Western Meadowlark	WEME	Common	Breeder	Native	179039
Passeriformes	Icteridae	Xanthocephalus xanthocephalus	Yellow-headed Blackbird	YHBL	Rare	Vagrant	Native	179043
Passeriformes	Laniidae	Lanius ludovicianus	Loggerhead Shrike	LOSH	Rare	Breeder	Native	178515
Passeriformes	Mimidae	Dumetella carolinensis	Gray Catbird	GRCA	Occasional	Vagrant	Native	178625
Passeriformes	Mimidae	Mimus polyglottos	Northern Mockingbird	NOMO	Uncommon	Breeder	Native	178620
Passeriformes	Mimidae	Oreoscoptes montanus	Sage Thrasher	SATH	Rare	Vagrant	Native	178654
Passeriformes	Mimidae	Toxostoma bendirei	Bendire's Thrasher	BETH	Occasional	Vagrant	Native	178636
Passeriformes	Mimidae	Toxostoma rufum	Brown Thrasher	BRTH	Occasional	Vagrant	Native	178627
Passeriformes	Motacillidae	Anthus cervinus	Red-throated Pipit	RTPI	Occasional	Vagrant	Native	178498
Passeriformes	Motacillidae	Anthus rubescens	American Pipit	AMPI	Occasional	Vagrant	Native	554127
Passeriformes	Parulidae	Dendroica caerulescens	Black-throated Blue Warbler	BTBW	Occasional	Vagrant	Native	178888
Passeriformes	Parulidae	Dendroica castanea	Bay-breasted Warbler	BBWA	Occasional	Vagrant	Native	178912
Passeriformes	Parulidae	Dendroica coronata	Yellow-rumped Warbler	YRWA	Common	Migratory	Native	178891
Passeriformes	Parulidae	Dendroica discolor	Prairie Warbler	PRWA	Occasional	Vagrant	Native	178918
Passeriformes	Parulidae	Dendroica dominica	Yellow-throated Warbler	YTWA	Occasional	Vagrant	Native	178905
Passeriformes	Parulidae	Dendroica fusca	Blackburnian Warbler	BLBW	Occasional	Vagrant	Native	178904
Passeriformes	Parulidae	Dendroica graciae	Grace's Warbler	GRWA	Occasional	Vagrant	Native	178909
Passeriformes	Parulidae	Dendroica magnolia	Magnolia Warbler	MAWA	Occasional	Vagrant	Native	178886
Passeriformes	Parulidae	Dendroica nigrescens	Black-throated Gray Warbler	BTYW	Rare	Vagrant	Native	178896
Passeriformes	Parulidae	Dendroica occidentalis	Hermit Warbler	HEWA	Common	Vagrant	Native	178902
Passeriformes	Parulidae	Dendroica palmarum	Palm Warbler	PAWA	Rare	Vagrant	Native	178921
Passeriformes	Parulidae	Dendroica pensilvanica	Chestnut-sided Warbler	CSWA	Occasional	Vagrant	Native	178911

Order	Family	Scientific name	Common name	Code	Abundance	Status	Origin	ID
Passeriformes	Parulidae	Dendroica petechia	Yellow Warbler	YWAR	Uncommon	Vagrant	Native	178878
Passeriformes	Parulidae	Dendroica striata	Blackpoll Warbler	BLPW	Rare	Vagrant	Native	178913
Passeriformes	Parulidae	Dendroica tigrina	Cape May Warbler	CMWA	Occasional	Vagrant	Native	178887
Passeriformes	Parulidae	Dendroica townsendi	Townsend's Warbler	TOWA	Uncommon	Vagrant	Native	178897
Passeriformes	Parulidae	Dendroica virens	Black-throated Green Warbler	BTNW	Occasional	Vagrant	Native	178898
Passeriformes	Parulidae	Geothlypis trichas	Common Yellowthroat	COYE	Uncommon	Migratory	Native	178944
Passeriformes	Parulidae	Icteria virens	Yellow-breasted Chat	YBCH	Uncommon	Vagrant	Native	178964
Passeriformes	Parulidae	Mniotilta varia	Black-and-white Warbler	BAWW	Rare	Vagrant	Native	178844
Passeriformes	Parulidae	Myioborus pictus	Painted Redstart	PARE	Occasional	Vagrant	Native	178986
Passeriformes	Parulidae	Oporornis formosus	Kentucky Warbler	KEWA	Occasional	Vagrant	Native	178937
Passeriformes	Parulidae	Oporornis philadelphia	Mourning Warbler	MOWA	Occasional	Vagrant	Native	178939
Passeriformes	Parulidae	Oporornis tolmiei	Macgillivray's Warbler	MGWA	Uncommon	Vagrant	Native	178940
Passeriformes	Parulidae	Parula americana	Northern Parula	NOPA	Occasional	Vagrant	Native	178868
Passeriformes	Parulidae	Protonotaria citrea	Prothonotary Warbler	PROW	Occasional	Vagrant	Native	178846
Passeriformes	Parulidae	Seiurus aurocapillus	Ovenbird	OVEN	Rare	Vagrant	Native	178927
Passeriformes	Parulidae	Seiurus noveboracensis	Northern Waterthrush	NOWA	Occasional	Vagrant	Native	178931
Passeriformes	Parulidae	Setophaga ruticilla	American Redstart	AMRE	Rare	Vagrant	Native	178979
Passeriformes	Parulidae	Vermivora celata	Orange-crowned Warbler	OCWA	Common	Breeder	Native	178856
Passeriformes	Parulidae	Vermivora luciae	Lucy's Warbler	LUWA	Occasional	Vagrant	Native	178866
Passeriformes	Parulidae	Vermivora peregrina	Tennessee Warbler	TEWA	Occasional	Vagrant	Native	178855
Passeriformes	Parulidae	Vermivora ruficapilla	Nashville Warbler	NAWA	Occasional	Vagrant	Native	178861
Passeriformes	Parulidae	Vermivora virginiae	Virginia's Warbler	VIWA	Occasional	Vagrant	Native	178864
Passeriformes	Parulidae	Wilsonia canadensis	Canada Warbler	CAWA	Occasional	Vagrant	Native	178977
Passeriformes	Parulidae	Wilsonia citrina	Hooded Warbler	HOOR	Occasional	Vagrant	Native	178972
Passeriformes	Parulidae	Wilsonia pusilla	Wilson's Warbler	WIWA	Common	Vagrant	Native	178973
Passeriformes	Passeridae	Passer domesticus	House Sparrow	HOSP	Rare	Vagrant	Native	179628
Passeriformes	Ptilogonatidae	Phainopepla nitens	Phainopepla	PHAI	Occasional	Breeder	Native	179877
Passeriformes	Regulidae	Regulus calendula	Ruby-crowned Kinglet	RCKI	Common	Migratory	Native	179870
Passeriformes	Regulidae	Regulus satrapa	Golden-crowned Kinglet	GCKI	Occasional	Migratory	Native	179865
Passeriformes	Sittidae	Sitta canadensis	Red-breasted Nuthatch	RBNU	Uncommon	Breeder	Native	178784
Passeriformes	Sittidae	Sitta carolinensis	White-breasted Nuthatch	WBNU	Occasional	Migratory	Native	178775
Passeriformes	Sturnidae	Sturnus vulgaris	European Starling	EUST	Abundant	Breeder	Non-Native	179637
Passeriformes	Thraupidae	Piranga ludoviciana	Western Tanager	WETA	Common	Vagrant	Native	179882
Passeriformes	Thraupidae	Piranga olivacea	Scarlet Tanager	SCTA	Occasional	Vagrant	Native	179883

Order	Family	Scientific name	Common name	Code	Abundance	Status	Origin	TSN
Passeriformes	Thraupidae	Piranga rubra	Summer Tanager	SUTA	Occasional	Migratory	Native	179888
Passeriformes	Troglodytidae	Catherpes mexicanus	Canyon Wren	CANW	Occasional	Resident	Native	178610
Passeriformes	Troglodytidae	Cistothorus palustris	Marsh Wren	MAWR	Occasional	Migratory	Native	178608
Passeriformes	Troglodytidae	Salpinctes obsoletus	Rock Wren	ROWR	Uncommon	Breeder	Native	178614
Passeriformes	Troglodytidae	Thryomanes bewickii	Bewick's Wren	BEWR	Common	Breeder	Native	178562
Passeriformes	Troglodytidae	Troglodytes aedon	House Wren	HOWR	Uncommon	Migratory	Native	178541
Passeriformes	Troglodytidae	Troglodytes pacificus	Pacific Wren	WIWR	Rare	Vagrant	Native	178547
Passeriformes	Turdidae	Catharus guttatus	Hermit Thrush	HETH	Occasional	Vagrant	Native	179779
Passeriformes	Turdidae	Catharus ustulatus	Swainson's Thrush	SWTH	Occasional	Breeder	Native	179788
Passeriformes	Turdidae	Myadestes townsendi	Townsend's Solitaire	TOSO	Occasional	Migratory	Native	179824
Passeriformes	Turdidae	Sialia currucoides	Mountain Bluebird	MOBL	Occasional	Migratory	Native	179811
Passeriformes	Turdidae	Sialia mexicana	Western Bluebird	WEBL	Occasional	Migratory	Native	179806
Passeriformes	Turdidae	Turdus migratorius	American Robin	AMRO	Occasional	Breeder	Native	179759
Passeriformes	Turdidae	Zoothera naevia	Varied Thrush	VATH	Rare	Migratory	Native	563804
Passeriformes	Tyrannidae	Contopus borealis	Olive-sided Flycatcher	OSFL	Uncommon	Vagrant	Native	178365
Passeriformes	Tyrannidae	Contopus sordidulus	Western Wood-Pewee	WEWP	Common	Vagrant	Native	178360
Passeriformes	Tyrannidae	Empidonax difficilis	Pacific-slope Flycatcher	PSFL	Common	Breeder	Native	178348
Passeriformes	Tyrannidae	Empidonax hammondii	Hammond's Flycatcher	HAFL	Rare	Vagrant	Native	554254
Passeriformes	Tyrannidae	Empidonax minimus	Least Flycatcher	LEFL	Occasional	Vagrant	Native	178344
Passeriformes	Tyrannidae	Empidonax oberholseri	Dusky Flycatcher	DUFL	Rare	Vagrant	Native	178346
Passeriformes	Tyrannidae	Empidonax traillii	Willow Flycatcher	WIFL	Uncommon	Vagrant	Native	178341
Passeriformes	Tyrannidae	Empidonax wrightii	Gray Flycatcher	GRFL	Rare	Vagrant	Native	178347
Passeriformes	Tyrannidae	Myiarchus cinerascens	Ash-throated Flycatcher	ATFL	Rare	Vagrant	Native	178316
Passeriformes	Tyrannidae	Pyrocephalus rubinus	Vermillion Flycatcher	VEFL	Occasional	Vagrant	Native	178371
Passeriformes	Tyrannidae	Sayornis nigricans	Black Phoebe	BLPH	Rare	Breeder	Native	178330
Passeriformes	Tyrannidae	Sayornis phoebe	Eastern Phoebe	EAPH	Occasional	Vagrant	Native	178329
Passeriformes	Tyrannidae	Sayornis saya	Say's Phoebe	SAPH	Common	Migratory	Native	178333
Passeriformes	Tyrannidae	Tyrannus forficatus	Scissor-tailed Flycatcher	STFL	Occasional	Vagrant	Native	178293
Passeriformes	Tyrannidae	Tyrannus tyrannus	Eastern Kingbird	EAKI	Occasional	Vagrant	Native	178279
Passeriformes	Tyrannidae	Tyrannus verticalis	Western Kingbird	WEKI	Uncommon	Vagrant	Native	178287
Passeriformes	Tyrannidae	Tyrannus vociferans	Cassin's Kingbird	CAKI	Rare	Vagrant	Native	178288
Passeriformes	Vireonidae	Vireo bellii	Bell's Vireo	BEVI	Occasional	Vagrant	Native	179003
Passeriformes	Vireonidae	Vireo cassinii	Cassin's Vireo	CAVI	Unknown	Unknown	Native	554456
Passeriformes	Vireonidae	Vireo gilvus	Warbling Vireo	WAVI	Uncommon	Migratory	Native	179023

Order	Family	Scientific name	Common name	Code	Abundance	Status	Origin	ID
Passeriformes	Vireonidae	Vireo huttoni	Hutton's Vireo	HUVI	Uncommon	Breeder	Native	178997
Passeriformes	Vireonidae	Vireo olivaceus	Red-eyed Vireo	REVI	Occasional	Vagrant	Native	179021
Passeriformes	Vireonidae	Vireo philadelphicus	Philadelphia Vireo	PHVI	Occasional	Vagrant	Native	179022
Passeriformes	Vireonidae	Vireo plumbeus	Plumbeus Vireo	PLVI	Unknown	Unknown	Native	554477
Passeriformes	Vireonidae	Vireo vicinior	Gray Vireo	GRVI	Occasional	Vagrant	Native	179008
Piciformes	Picidae	Colaptes auratus	Northern Flicker	NOFL	Uncommon	Breeder	Native	178154
Piciformes	Picidae	Melanerpes formicivorus	Acorn Woodpecker	ACWO	Uncommon	Breeder	Native	178189
Piciformes	Picidae	Melanerpes lewis	Lewis' Woodpecker	LEWO	Uncommon	Unknown	Native	178196
Piciformes	Picidae	Picoides nuttallii	Nuttall's Woodpecker	NUWO	Occasional	Vagrant	Native	178258
Piciformes	Picidae	Sphyrapicus nuchalis	Red-naped Sapsucker	RNSA	Occasional	Vagrant	Native	178211
Piciformes	Picidae	Sphyrapicus ruber	Red-breasted Sapsucker	RBSA	Uncommon	Migratory	Native	178212
Piciformes	Picidae	Sphyrapicus varius	Yellow-bellied Sapsucker	YBSA	Rare	Migratory	Native	178202
Strigiformes	Caprimulgidae	Chordeiles acutipennis	Lesser Nighthawk	LENI	Uncommon	Vagrant	Native	177988
Strigiformes	Caprimulgidae	Chordeiles minor	Common Nighthawk	CONI	Occasional	Vagrant	Native	177979
Strigiformes	Caprimulgidae	Phalaenoptilus nuttallii	Common Poorwill	COPO	Uncommon	Vagrant	Native	555544
Strigiformes	Strigidae	Aegolius acadicus	Northern Saw-whet Owl	NSWO	Uncommon	Breeder	Native	177942
Strigiformes	Strigidae	Asio flammeus	Short-eared Owl	SEOW	Occasional	Breeder	Native	177935
Strigiformes	Strigidae	Asio otus	Long-eared Owl	LEOW	Rare	Migratory	Native	177932
Strigiformes	Strigidae	Athene cunicularia	Burrowing Owl	BUOW	Occasional	Breeder	Native	177946
Strigiformes	Strigidae	Bubo virginianus	Great Horned Owl	GHOW	Occasional	Vagrant	Native	177884
Strigiformes	Strigidae	Otus flammeolus	Flammulated Owl	FLOW	Occasional	Vagrant	Native	177878
Strigiformes	Tytonidae	Tyto alba	Barn Owl	BANO	Rare	Breeder	Native	177851

Appendix B: Island-specific status of breeding birds

Island codes are SM = San Miguel, SR = Santa Rosa, SC = Santa Cruz, AN = East Anacapa, and SB = Santa Barbara. Breeding status codes are B = regular breeder, O = occasional breeder. Species marked by asterisks are endemic to one or more islands. Data sources are Jones et al. (1999), Latta et al. (2005), and Coonan et al. (2010).

Common Name	Latin Name	Code	AN	SB	SC	SM	SR
Great Blue Heron	*Ardea herodias*	GRHE			B		B
Golden Eagle	*Aquila chrysaetos*	GOEA			O		O
Red-tailed Hawk	*Buteo jamaicensis*	RTHA	B		B	B	B
Northern Harrier	*Circus cyaneus*	NOHA				O	O
Bald Eagle	*Haliaeetus leucocephalus*	BAEA	B		O		B
Peregrine Falcon	*Falco peregrinus*	PEFA	B	B	B	B	B
American Kestrel	*Falco sparverius*	AMKE	B	B	B	B	B
California Quail	*Callipepla californica*	CAQU			B		B
Mourning Dove	*Zenaida macroura*	MODO		O	B		B
Barn Owl	*Tyto alba*	BANO	B	B	B	B	B
Northern Waw-whet Owl	*Aegolius acadicus*	NSWO			B		
Short-eared Owl	*Asio flammeus*	SEOW		B			
Burrowing Owl	*Athene cunicularia*	BUOW		B			
White-throated Swift	*Aeronautes saxatalis*	WTSW	B		B		B
Anna's Hummingbird	*Calypte anna*	ANHU			B	B	
Allen's Hummingbird **	*Selasphorus sasin*	ALHU	B		B	B	B
Northern Flicker	*Colaptes auratus*	NOFL			B		
Acorn Woodpecker	*Melanerpes formicivorus*	ACWO			B		
Pacific-slope Flycatcher **	*Empidonax difficilis*	PSFL	B		B		B
Black Phoebe	*Sayornis nigricans*	BLPH			B	O	B
Ash-throated Flycatcher	*Myiarchus cinerascens*	ATFL			B		
Horned Lark **	*Eremophila alpestris*	HOLA		B	B	B	B
Barn Swallow	*Hirundo rustica*	BARS	B	B	B	B	B
Island Scrub-jay **	*Aphelocoma insularis*	ISSJ			B		
Common Raven	*Corvus corax*	CORA			B		B
Red-breasted Nuthatch	*Sitta canadensis*	RBNU			B		
Canyon Wren	*Catherpes mexicanus*	CANW			O		
Rock Wren	*Salpinctes obsoletus*	ROWR	B	B	B	B	B
Bewick's Wren **	*Thryomanes bewickii*	BEWR	B		B		B
Blue-gray Gnatcatcher	*Polioptila caerulea*	BGGN			B		
Northern Mockingbird	*Mimus polyglottos*	NOMO			B		B
Loggerhead Shrike **	*Lanius ludovicianus*	LOSH			B		B
European Sstarling	*Sturnus vulgaris*	EUST					B
Hutton's Vireo	*Vireo huttoni*	HUVI	B		B		B
Orange-crowned Warbler**	*Vermivora celata*	OCWA	B	B	B	B	B
Black-headed Grosbeak	*Pheucticus melanocephalus*	BHGR			B		
Rufous-crowned Sparrow**	*Aimophila ruficeps*	RCSP	B		B		
Grasshopper Sparrow	*Ammodramus savannarum*	GRSP			B		
Song Sparrow **	*Melospiza melodia*	SOSP			B	B	B
Spotted Towhee **	*Pipilo maculates*	SPTO			B		B
Chipping Wparrow	*Spizella passerine*	CHSP	B		B		B
Western Meadowlark	*Sturnella neglecta*	WEME	B	B	B	B	B
Lesser Goldfinch	*Carduelis psaltria*	LEGO			B	O	B
House Finch **	*Carpodacus mexicanus*	HOFI	B		B	B	B
Total Number of Species			17	11	39	16	30

41

Standard Operating Procedures (SOPs)

The following SOPs are attached at the end of this document and are numbered individually to facilitate using them independently and revising or updating them.

Channel Islands National Park Landbird Monitoring Protocol
Standard Operating Procedure (SOP)
SOP # 1: Before the Field Season
Version 1.00 (2011)

Revision History Log:

Prev. Version #	Revision Date	Author	Changes Made	Reason for Change	New Version #

This Standard Operating Procedure (SOP) describes pre-season procedures for monitoring landbirds at Channel Islands National Park (CHIS). Landbird monitoring at CHIS is managed by the Landbird Program Manager and is conducted by Resources Management (RM) Inventory and Monitoring (I&M) staff. Before conducting surveys, observers should review the entire CHIS landbird protocol narrative; including SOPs and appendices This SOP describes general pre-season preparation, scheduling considerations, and supplies and equipment needs.

General Preparation and Review

Prior knowledge of species likely to be encountered on the Channel Islands is the key in preparing for the birding season. Observers should review the list of CHIS bird species in the current CHIS Checklist (Appendix A) and island-specific breeding status table (Appendix B), and note the alphabetical codes for species frequently encountered on each island. Copies of species lists can be used in the field for reference. The species list is also contained in the LB.mdb database.

Waypoints for each point-count station along a transect, or waypoints for the beginning and end of a line transect (trail), must be loaded into the GPS unit prior to the start of the field season. Waypoints, which are the X and Y coordinates for each point-count station, are used to navigate to their location. SOP #3 contains a list of point locations for all CHIS sampling locations and transects. Waypoints for transects also will be stored as part of the project metadata.

Scheduling Field Work

1. Breeding bird surveys will be conducted during the period that coincides with the peak-breeding activity of most birds (March through June, starting in March for the southern islands). Specific survey dates may vary slightly because of weather, island road conditions and other island conditions. The sampling window will be documented each year with metadata notes on unusual events. Sampling dates should be scheduled, and sampling logistics organized prior to the start of each field season.

2. Santa Barbara and East Anacapa Islands can be sampled in one tour by one observer. San Miguel Island can be usually be sampled by two observers in one tour depending on fog and wind conditions. Santa Rosa Island sampling requires two observers for up to six tours, depending on weather and road conditions.

Table SOP 1-2. Annual field schedule for landbird monitoring at Channel Islands National Park.

Island	Survey Date Interval
Santa Barbara	Early March
East Anacapa	Early to mid-March
San Miguel	Mid-March to early June
Santa Rosa	Mid-March to early June

Organizing Supplies and Equipment

See Table SOP 1-1 for a list of equipment needed prior to commencing field work. Equipment should be organized and made ready several weeks before the field season.

Table SOP 1-1. List of equipment needed before commencing field work.

Number Needed	Description
1	Timepiece; suitable to time count
1	Binoculars
1	Declination-adjustable compass with sighting capability (i.e. a mirror)
1	Lasar range finder
1	MP3 player for listening to bird calls and songs
1	GPS unit for navigating to bird plots
As needed	Master list of four-letter bird codes for all species likely to be encountered, specifically noting the breeding target species
As needed	Data forms (copied onto non 100% recycled substantial paper)
2 - 3	At least two writing utensils, in case you lose one (pencil or indelible ink pen)
1	Clip boards for recording data and carrying data sheet
1	Vest for carrying equipment (backpack and hip packs may be substituted)
As needed	Reference book for bird identification
As needed	Insect repellent, sunscreen
As needed	Sunglasses
1	Field first aid kit

Suggested Readings and Audio References

The following reference material should be reviewed and carried into the field for bird identification background information:

- An information package containing the protocol with SOPS, site waypoint coordinates, island field maps and detailed site description information, bird code lists, and CHIS bird checklist.

- Sibley, David Allen. 2003. The Sibley field guide to birds of western North America. Alfred A. Knopf, New York.

- Thayer Guide to the Birds of North America software.

- Peterson, R. T. 1999. Peterson field guides: Western Bird Songs software produced by Cornell Laboratory of Ornithology and Interactive Audio. Houghlin Mifflin Co., Boston.

Channel Islands National Park Landbird Monitoring Protocol

Standard Operating Procedure (SOP)

SOP # 2: Training Observers
Version 1.00 (2011)

Revision History Log:

Prev. Version #	Revision Date	Author	Changes Made	Reason for Change	New Version #

This Standard Operating Procedure (SOP) explains the training procedures that all observers should follow to learn (1) how to identify birds by sight and vocalizations, and (2) how to estimate distances in the field.

Identification of Birds by Sight and Vocalizations
The most essential component for the collection of credible, high-quality bird data is well-trained and experienced observers. This cannot be overemphasized. Various studies have shown that observer bias is one of the most noteworthy bias factors in trend analysis of landbird populations (Kepler and Scott 1981, Baker and Sauer 1995). Training should ensure that all observers are able to identify, by sight and sound, all of the bird species expected to be encountered in the parks and >90% of bird species that have reasonable potential to occur in the area. It is also essential that observers are able to accurately and consistently estimate distances to birds and follow standard operating procedures to ensure data quality across time. In point-transect counts, most birds are recorded aurally. Therefore, it is important to hire observers with good hearing ability to ensure consistent data collection (Ramsey and Scott 1981). The analysis of distance-sampling and occupancy data can account for differences in observer skill by using Observer as a covariate, but the ability to model these differences has limitations. Observers must be prepared both mentally and physically for the extreme weather conditions and difficult terrain of Channel Islands National Park.

Procedures:

1. See Appendix A for the master list of bird species that may be encountered at Channel Islands National Park, as well as the island-specific overview of species known to breed on one or more of the Channel Islands (Appendix B). Beginning several months prior to the field-season, review and practice bird identification skills. Become familiar with the 4-character alphabetical codes for species frequently encountered on the islands.

2. Birders should pass a minimum proficiency test on the vocalizations and sight ID of bird species likely to be encountered, correctly identifying all common species likely to be

encountered and 90% of the less frequently encountered species (i.e., species encountered less than five times annually).

3. Regardless of skill level, birders should spend time in the field familiarizing themselves with the birds in the park prior to starting a survey.

4. Suggested reference materials for conducting bird surveys at Channel Islands National Park:

   - Tapes or CDs of bird songs for species found in southern California. These tapes and CDs are produced by Cornell Laboratory of Ornithology's Library of Natural Sounds.
   - Thayer Guide to the Birds of North America software.
   - Bird slides of species likely to be encountered can be obtained from Cornell Laboratory of Ornithology.
   - Sibley, David Allen. 2003. The Sibley field guide to birds of western North America. Alfred A. Knopf, New York.

Estimating Distances to Birds Seen or Heard

Training to estimate distances to birds should follow a series of steps. For observers who are already competent at identifying birds by sight and sound, one full day of training following these guidelines is usually all that is necessary to be able to estimate distances within 10%. Surveyors recalibrate themselves the afternoon before a bird survey begins.

1. Begin by placing flagging at 10 m, 25 m, 50 m, and 100 m from a central point and having observers estimate distances to trees, rocks, and flagging from the "station."

2. Have each observer place flagging at four or five locations visible from the station, and then have everyone in the group record distances to each flag in a field book. Distances should be estimated to the nearest meter. Then, use a tape measure or laser rangefinder to measure the distance to each flag, and have each person compare his or her initial estimate to the actual distance. Repeat this exercise at several sites with both open and closed vegetation until observers can consistently estimate distances to within 10% of the actual distance.

3. Half of the group should place themselves at various distances away from the station, and quietly wait until a bird vocalizes near them. The other half of the group should remain at the station, and estimate the distance to any birds that vocalize. Horizontal distances should be estimated, as if a plumb bob was lowered to the ground from the bird's location. If possible, observers should visually identify the tree or branch where they think the bird is, and estimate the horizontal distance to an object that they can see directly below where they think the bird is vocalizing. If the vegetation is too thick to see the tree or shrub, the observer should not move around to get a better view, but rather estimate the distance from where they are standing. The observer closest to the bird should then indicate where the bird was vocalizing from and measure the distance to the point directly under the bird from the station using a tape measure or laser rangefinder. This is a slow but important part of the training and should be repeated until observers have experience with estimating distances to a number of different species and call or song types.

4. Continue distance estimation training during simultaneous point count surveys and land transects. Divide observers into small groups (five people or fewer) and conduct counts from the same location. At the end of each count, have the observers compare notes and discuss any discrepancies in the species detected and the estimated distances. Remember that the distance to where the bird was first detected should be recorded, so if a bird flies towards the station, the distance where it was first heard or seen is recorded, not the closest distance or where it lands. Continue these simultaneous counts until there is consistency among observers with regards to the species and distances recorded.

Literature Cited

Baker, R. J. and J. R. Sauer. 1995. Statistical aspects of point count sampling. Pages 125-130 in C. J. Ralph, J. R. Sauer and S. Droege, eds. Monitoring bird populations by point counts, USDA Forest Service, Pacific Southwest Research Station, General Technical Report PSW-GTR-149.

Kepler, C. B. and J. M. Scott. 1981. Reducing bird count variability by training observers. Studies in Avian Biology 6:366-371.

Ramsey, F. L., and J. M. Scott. 1981. Tests of hearing ability. Studies in Avian Biology 6:341–345.

Locations of Point Count Stations and Line Transects
Version 1.00 (2011)

Revision History Log:

Prev. Version #	Revision Date	Author	Changes Made	Reason for Change	New Version #

Landbird monitoring has been conducted annually at Channel Islands National Park since 1993. The original landbird monitoring protocol comprised line transects on the smaller islands (San Miguel, East Anacapa, and Santa Barbara) and point count transects on the much larger island of Santa Rosa. In April of 2000, after 8 years of annual monitoring, the landbird monitoring program was reviewed by a team of subject-matter experts to determine whether the monitoring was still meeting the primary management and monitoring objectives, and to review the methods and level of change that could be detected by the level of monitoring that was being done. One of the primary management questions that the park managers wanted to answer was, "As the vegetation on the islands recovers from the effects of overgrazing and other historical land use practices, how do the bird populations respond?" This key management question could not adequately be answered because a single line transect survey would cover multiple vegetation types on a particular island, and bird species composition or density could not be analyzed by vegetation type. The program review recommended shifting entirely to point counts, which would be randomly located, separated by 250 m, and stratified by habitat type on each island. The development of new landbird monitoring methods began in 2001, based on recommendations from the program review, and the final siting of new point count counting stations was completed in 2003. To help provide a "crosswalk" between the data collected using the older and newer sampling design, all previously-monitored line transect and point counts were conducted on Santa Barbara, East Anacapa, Santa Rosa and San Miguel Islands for a 3-year period while at the same time we began sampling of the 226 newly-established point count sites on the four islands (33 on Santa Barbara, 8 on East Anacapa, 145 on Santa Rosa and 40 on San Miguel).

The locations of sampling points on the 3 smaller islands were determined using a geographic information system (GIS) analysis that randomly placed point count stations on each island, but which excluded developed areas, areas within 100 m of a road, and areas that were too steep to safely access. Minor adjustments to some of the randomly-selected locations were made so that all point count stations were at least 250 m apart to avoid sampling the same birds. The location of final point sites was completed in 2003 after some initial pilot sampling. The locations of all point count and line transect monitoring sites are summarized below in Table SOP 3-1.

Table SOP 3-1. Locations and description of line transect and point count sampling stations used for monitoring landbirds at Channel Islands National Park.

Island	Site Code	Site Name	Type	Habitat	Directions	Habitat Notes
AN	AE01	LBAE1	PC	COR		
AN	AE02	LBAE2	PC	ICE		
AN	AE03	LBAE3	PC	COR		
AN	AE04	LBAE4	PC	GRS		
AN	AE05	LBAE5	PC	COR		
AN	AE06	LBAE6	PC	GRS		
AN	AE07	LBAE7	PC	COR		
AN	AE08	LBAE8	PC	COR		
AN	AN01	LBAN01COR	PC	UNK		
AN	AN07	LBANO7GRS	PC	UNK		
AN	TRLS	East Anacapa	LT	COR		
SB	ARCH	Arch Point Loop	LT	GRS		
SB	BX01	Boxthorn 01	PC	BOX		
SB	CNYN	Canyons	LT	COR		
SB	CO01	Coreopsis 01	PC	COR		
SB	CO02	Coreopsis 02	PC	COR		
SB	CO03	Coreopsis 03	PC	COR		
SB	CO04	Coreopsis 04	PC	COR		
SB	CO05	Coreopsis 05	PC	COR		
SB	CO06	Coreopsis 06	PC	COR		
SB	CO07	Coreopsis 07	PC	COR		
SB	CO08	Coreopsis 08	PC	COR		
SB	CO09	Coreopsis 09	PC	COR		
SB	ELSL	Elephant Seal Cove Tr	LT	SBL		
SB	GR01	Grassland 01	PC	GRS		
SB	GR02	Grassland 02	PC	GRS		
SB	SB01	LBSB01	PC	GRS	located approximately 50m W/above trail to Arch Point, just before first ravine.	90% low grass; 8% FIHE/herbs/misc.; 2% crystalline ICPL.

Island	Site Code	Site Name	Type	Habitat	Directions	Habitat Notes
SB	SB02	LBSB02	PC	COR	Stake in small COR shrub between and near low red aluminum stake and LV stake to W.	40% COR, 30% GRS, 5% herbs, 5% SBL, 5% BUWH
SB	SB03	LBSB03	PC	ICE	near cliff - out of BRPE nesting areas; stake in SBL shrub;	40% ICE, 30% GRS, 25% SBL, 5% herbs
SB	SB04	LBSB04	PC	GRS	located approx. 200m W of trail and approx. 200m E of bare spot on hill; on the S fringe of scaterred COR; N of VEGSBI 9; approx. 25m NW would be in COR. Occasional BRPE nesting in the area.	80% GRS; 15% COR; 5%herbs
SB	SB05	LBSB05	PC	GRS	The stake is located in a COR bush about 15m west of trail between switchbacks.	Habitat consists of 95% grass and 5% low herbs, with an occ. COR bush.
SB	SB06	LBSB06	PC	SBL		70% GRS, 20% SBL, 5% herbs, 5% ICE
SB	SB07	LBSB07	PC	GRS	W of trail up N Peak 73m.	80% GRS, 20% herbs
SB	SB08	LBSB08	PC	GRS	25m east of trail - stake in COR bush.	90% GRS; 5% herbs, 5% COR.
SB	SB09	LBSB09	PC	COR	5" w of trail, in COR stand behind COR plant.	50% COR, 30% GRS, 10% shrub, 5% herbs, 5% Opuntia (Prickly Pear Cactus).
SB	SB10	LBSB10	PC	SBL		70% GRS, 20% SBL, 5% ICE, 5% herbs.
SB	SB11	LBSB11	PC	GRS	N. of old trail,	95% GRS, 5% herbs.
SB	SB12	LBSB12	PC	SBL	Stake in Shrub.	60% GRS, 15% ICE, 20% SBL, 5% herbs.
SB	SB13	LBSB13	PC	CAC	located NE down old trail to top of cactus in Cave Canyon. SE owl located @ NE end of canyon.	SP consists of 40% CAC, 10% COR, and 50% GRS/fitle with occasional BXTH.
SB	SB14	LBSB14	PC	COR	located on S side Cave Canyon at lip in view of picnic tables, 200m W.	80% COR; 20% GRS/herb.
SB	SB15	LBSB15	PC	GRS	Stake in low grass, visible from Saddle.	95% GRS, 5% herbs.
SB	SB16	LBSB16	PC	GRS	located + or - 35m NW of trail just S of drainage, between Cave and Middle Canyons, E of Coreopsis on hill.	SP consists of 99% GRS, 1% BXTH and occasional BLDI
SB	SB17	LBSB17	PC	CAC	N Side of mouth of Cave Canyon.	40% PRPE cactus, 30% COR, 25% GRS, 5% herbs.
SB	SB18	LBSB18	PC	BOX	located close to top, not saddle. Approximately 30m S of Ridge Trial to North Peak from Saddle.	SP consists of 99% GRS, 10% fitle and BLDI/herbs.
SB	SB19	LBSB19	PC	COR	located on south side of lower middle Cave Canyon, facing N.	25% COR, 25% GRS, 25% BXTH, 20% PRPE, 5% herbs.
SB	SB20	LBSB20	PC	GRS	located on the south side of Middle Canyon Rim at cliff.	75% GRS, 10% COR, 10% BXTH, 5% herbs.
SB	SB21	LBSB21	PC	GRS	Stake 5m W of trail in BXTH bush.	80% GRS, 15% BXTH, 5% herbs.
SB	SB22	LBSB22	PC	GRS	located N of Graveyard Canyon and E of large Cactus patc, 150m E of trail.	Consists of 85% grass, 5% CAC, 5% BXTH, 5% fitle and herbs

Island	Site Code	Site Name	Type	Habitat	Directions	Habitat Notes
SB	SB23	LBSB23	PC	GRS	Near bench above Saddle,	90% GRS, 10% herbs
SB	SB24	LBSB24	PC	COR	The stake is located NW of the Badlands, 33m W of Coreopsis Forrest. The habitat consists of	45% COR, 45% GRS, and 5% shrubs, 5% herbs..
SB	SB25	LBSB25	PC	GRS	225m from 33 at cliff edge in Graveyard Cyn (south side); neat BRPE nest habitat.	65% GRS, 15% bare, 15% COR, 5% herbs.
SB	SB26	LBSB26	PC	SCL	250m W of 33, stake in sage 10m east of site at cliff edge.	30% GRS, 15% Rock/lichen cliff, 15% BUWH, 15% sage, 10% herbs.
SB	SB27	LBSB27	PC	GRS	located near cliff moved 5m inland awy from cliff, N of small ravine and E of Badlands; approximately 75m E of trail.	Consisits of 85% grass, 5% bare % ice plant, 5% low herbs/SBL.
SB	SB28	LBSB28	PC	SBL	The stake is north of 3 gullies off peak to west. The habitat consists of	40% SBL, 40% GRS, 10% ICE, 5% herbs, 5% bare.
SB	SB29	LBSB29	PC	ICE		60% GRS, 25% ICE, 10% SBL, 5% herbs.
SB	SB30	LBSB30	PC	GRS		
SB	SB31	LBSB31	PC	GRS	E of bare drainage on hillside; closest to S side of Badlands; + or - 100m E of trail.	Habitat consists of 85% GRS, and 10% BXTH and 5% herbs
SB	SB32	LBSB32	PC	ICE	The stake is located near the badlands and Coreopsis forest.	50% ICE, 25% GRS, 20% SBL, 5% herbs.
SB	SB33	LBSB33	PC	GRS		
SB	SC01	?	PC	UNK		
SB	SGNL	Signal Peak Loop	LT	GRS		
SC	SCP1	Prisoners 1	PC	DSS		
SC	SCP2	Prisoners 2	PC	RIW		
SC	SCP3	Prisoners 3	PC	CSS		
SC	SCP4	Prisoners 4	PC	MXW		
SC	SCP5	Prisoners 5	PC	RIP		
SC	SCP6	Prisoners 6	PC	MXW		
SC	SCP7	Prisoners 7	PC	RIP		
SC	SCP8	Prisoners 8	PC	MXW		
SM	HRRS	Harris Point	LT	LUP		
SM	LKBD	Dry Lakebed	LT	GRS		
SM	NDVR	Nidever Canyon	LT	COR		
SM	SM01	LBSM1	PC	BAC		

Island	Site Code	Site Name	Type	Habitat	Directions	Habitat Notes
SM	SM02	LBSM2	PC	CSS		
SM	SM03	LBSM3	PC	CAL		
SM	SM04	LBSM4	PC	RIW		
SM	SM05	LBSM5	PC	COR		
SM	SM06	LBSM6	PC	LUP		
SM	SM07	LBSM7	PC	LUP		
SM	SM08	LBSM8	PC	GRS		
SM	SM09	LBSM9	PC	LUP		
SM	SM10	LBSM10	PC	LUP	SM10 lies 325 m NW of SM11. Cross the small canyon to the W of SM11 (it is within the 50m radius). Stay to the S to avoid the next canyon. Once past it, follow the GPS direction (NW) to the point. The stake is	75%LUPI, 15%ICPL, 10%HERBS (ISOC, ASMI).
SM	SM11	LBSM11	PC	CSX	Head up the Cross Island Trail (CIT) until perpendicular with the point. You should be past the tall wooden stake on the right side of the trail. Travel on the south side of all canyons. About 400 m from	40%LUPI, 30%BACC, 10%HERBS, 10%ISOC, 10% LOCO.
SM	SM12	LBSM12	PC	LUP	Near Nidever mouse and veg grids.	75% LUPI, 15%BACC, 10%HERBS (ISOC, LOCO, DUDL).
SM	SM13	LBSM13	PC	CSX	From SM18, cross small ravine directly to E of point, then cut up towards the ridgeline. The hill there is steep, but hikeable. Follow GPS once the top is reached. About 300m SE of Cross Island Tr	25%ISOC, 25%LOCO, 20%GRS, 15%ICPL, 10% MOGL, 5%HERBS.
SM	SM14	LBSM14	PC	RIH		35%RIP, 25%BARE, 25%CORI, 15%HERBS.
SM	SM15	LBSM15	PC	CSX	Stay on Cross Island Trail until well past the weather station. When point lies directly S of trail, turn off and go direct to point.	25% Locoweed; 25% GRS; 20% Haplo; 5%Morning Glory; 20% ICE; 5% mixed herbs.
SM	SM16	LBSM16	PC	CBL	Tough to get to. On the flats, at the bottom of the ridgeline. Follow GPS from SM16 (SE) to the cliffs. A large ravine begins towards the E, heading S down to the flats. Stay on the W side of that ravine until the	25%LOCO, 20%ISOC, 20%ICPL, 20% GRS, 10%BACC, 5% HERBS
SM	SM17	LBSM17	PC	LUP	0.13m E of SM17;Easy walk from 17. 7m elevation	70%LUPI, 15%ICPL, 10%GRS, 5% HERBS.
SM	SM18	LBSM18	PC	GRS		95% GRS; 5%hergbs.
SM	SM19	LBSM19	PC	COR	Approx 50 m from Cabrillo monument.	80% CORI, 10% HERBS (LOCO, SEDA, BKWH, LUPI, ISOC), 5% GRS, 5% BACC.

Island	Site Code	Site Name	Type	Habitat	Directions	Habitat Notes
SM	SM20	LBSM20	PC	COR		40% CORI, 20%ROCK, 15% LOCO, 10%DUDL, 10%ISOC & CAST, 5% HERBS (BACC, NEPH)
SM	SM21	LBSM21	PC	COR		50%CORI, 20%LUPI, 10%BACC, 10%HERBS(ISOC, ASMI), 5% GRS, 5% ICPL.
SM	SM22	LBSM22	PC	CSX		40% CORI, 30%Bare, 30% MXED (CAST, ISOC, BKWH, LOCO)
SM	SM23	LBSM23	PC	COR	Approx. 600m NE of SM 24. Line from SM24 goes through thick Coreopsis and Dudley habitat, so care is needed. In the caliche area, there is a prominent rectangular piece of caliche. The	35%CORI, 20% GRS, 15% LOCO, 15% ISOC, 5% DUDL, 5% BKWT, 5% HERBS.
SM	SM24	LBSM24	PC	GRS		
SM	SM25	LBSM25	PC	GRS	Straight line from SM27. Point is on the E side of small ravine, and should be easily visible from the W side. There is a flat place to cross the ravine very near the stake.	95%GRS, 5% HERBS. 50%Mixed CAST, CORI, ARTE, LOCO, ISOC, BKWH,MOGL, 35% GRS, 15% BACC
SM	SM26	LBSM26	PC	COR	Straight line from 28, crosses CPT. Point is not far off trail (NE).	70%GRS, 15%ISOC, 10%BACC, 5% HERBS.
SM	SM27	LBSM27	PC	GRS	Very easy walk through tall grass from SM29.	80%GRS,15%BACC, 5% HERBS.
SM	SM28	LBSM28	PC	GRS	Follow trail from SM2 E, towards Brooks Site Middle. Once near the last pen, it will be necessary to go off trail to get to the point. It is on the E side of the large ravine.	80%GRS, 15% ISOC, 5% CORI, 10%ICEP.
SM	SM29	LBSM29	PC	GRS		30%CORI, 30% BACC, 15%ISOC, 15% GRS, 10% HERBS NEED
SM	SM30	LBSM30	PC	COR	Go up SM hill until past the lupine field, then head around the hill. Stay S of the caliche. Once around the N facing side of the hill, and past the caliche, follow the GPS	40% ARTE, 20% GAYA, 20% Bare, 10%GRS, 10% HERBS. SM31 lies 1.25 km SW of SM9.
SM	SM31	LBSM31	PC	CSS	There are 2 options. The first is to go around the base of GM. There is a large canyon on the other side of the mountain, so once you reach it, go up GM until you can cross over. Proceed by GPS directio	60% GRS, 40% BACC. SM32 lies 1.7km SSE of SM34.
SM	SM32	LBSM2	PC	GRS	SM33 lies 1.66km NW of SM31. Head NNW away from GM canyon until level. Then follow GPS direction (NW) to go around the base of GM. Stay low on the shoulder of the mountain. You shoul	20% GRS, 20% ICPL, 15% LOCO, 15% ISOC, 10%LUPI, 10%BACC, 10% HERBS.
SM	SM33	LB33	PC	CSX		

Island	Site Code	Site Name	Type	Habitat	Directions	Habitat Notes
SM	SM34	LBSM34	PC	COR	Follow GPS direction. The stake is on the point of the covergence of 2 canyons. Be careful of Coreopsis on the way.	30%CORI, 30%BACC, 20%ICPL, 15% HERBS, 5%Bare. SM34 lies 660m WNW of SM33.
SM	SM35	LBSM35	PC	GRS		70%GRS, 20%ICPL, 10%HERBS.
SM	SM36	LBSM36	PC	GRS		70% GRS, 20% ICPL, 10%HERBS
SM	SM37	LBSM37	PC	LUP		75% LUPI, 20% ICPL, 3% HERBS, 2% BACC
SM	SM38	LBSM38	PC	LUP		45%LUPI, 40% GRS, 10%ICPL, 5% HERBS
SM	SM39	LBSM39	PC	GRS		75% GRS, 5% LUPI, 5%ISOC, 5%ICPL, 10%HERBS.
SM	SM40	LBSM40	PC	CAL		35%Bare, 35%GRS, 10%ISOC, 10% ICPL, 10%HERBS.
SM	SMHL	San Miguel Hill	LT	BAC		
SM	WLLW	Willow Canyon	LT	BAC		
SR	CC01	Cherry Canyon 01	PC	CHA		
SR	CC02	Cherry Canyon 02	PC	CHA		
SR	CC03	Cherry Canyon 03	PC	CHA		
SR	CC04	Cherry Canyon 04	PC	CHA		
SR	CC05	Cherry Canyon 05	PC	CHA		
SR	EM01	Estuary/Marsh 1	LT	MAR		
SR	EM02	Estuary/Marsh 2	LT	MAR		
SR	IO01	Island Oak 01	PC	OAK		
SR	IO02	Island Oak 02	PC	OAK		
SR	IO03	Island Oak 03	PC	OAK		
SR	IO04	Island Oak 04	PC	OAK		
SR	IO05	Island Oak 05	PC	OAK		
SR	IO06	Island Oak 06	PC	OAK		
SR	IO07	Island Oak 07	PC	OAK		
SR	IO08	Island Oak 08	PC	OAK		
SR	IO09	Island Oak 09	PC	OAK		
SR	LC01	Lobos Canyon 01	PC	RIP		
SR	LC02	Lobos Canyon 02	PC	RIP		
SR	LC03	Lobos Canyon 03	PC	RIP		

Island	Site Code	Site Name	Type	Habitat	Directions	Habitat Notes
SR	LC04	Lobos Canyon 04	PC	RIP		
SR	LC05	Lobos Canyon 05	PC	RIP		
SR	LC06	Lobos Canyon 06	PC	RIP		
SR	LC07	Lobos Canyon 07	PC	RIP		
SR	LC08	Lobos Canyon 08	PC	RIP		
SR	LC09	Lobos Canyon 09	PC	RIP		
SR	LC10	Lobos Canyon 10	PC	RIP		
SR	LC11	Lobos Canyon 11	PC	RIP		
SR	LC12	Lobos Canyon 12	PC	RIP		
SR	LC13	Lobos Canyon 13	PC	RIP		
SR	LC14	Lobos Canyon 14	PC	RIP		
SR	LC15	Lobos Canyon 15	PC	RIP		
SR	LC16	Lobos Canyon 16	PC	RIP		
SR	LC17	Lobos Canyon 17	PC	RIP		
SR	LC18	Lobos Canyon 18	PC	RIP		
SR	LC19	Lobos Canyon 19	PC	RIP		
SR	LC20	Lobos Canyon 20	PC	RIP		
SR	SR001	LBSR1	PC	CSS		
SR	SR002	LBSR2	PC	GRS		
SR	SR003	LBSR3	PC	GRS		
SR	SR004	LBSR4	PC	GRS		
SR	SR005	LBSR5	PC	GRS		
SR	SR006	LBSR6	PC	CHA		
SR	SR007	LBSR7	PC	GRS		
SR	SR008	LBSR8	PC	GRS		
SR	SR009	LBSR9	PC	GRS		
SR	SR010	LBSR10	PC	MXW		50% TOY, 35% BACC/SAGE, 5% GRS, 5% ROCK, 5% HERBS.
SR	SR011	LBSR11	PC	CSS		50%GRS, 45%BACC/SAGE, 5% HERBS, 1 TOY.
SR	SR012	LBSR12	PC	GRS		95%GRS, 5%HERBS, OCC BACC.

Island	Site Code	Site Name	Type	Habitat	Directions	Habitat Notes
SR	SR013	LBSR13	PC	CSS		75%SAGE/BACC, 15%FERN, 5%GRS, 5%HERBS.
SR	SR014	LBSR14	PC	GRS		60%GRS, 30%BACC, 10%HERBS.
SR	SR015	LBSR15	PC	GRS	ark near campground kiosk. Cross fence (there is a gate at correr NE of kiosk), head E of kiosk. Stay on N side of ravine. Stake is about 1/4 of the way down bank.	50%GRS, 30%CSS, 10%BACC, 10% HERBS.
SR	SR016	LBSR16	PC	RIP	Somewhat steep. From 16, go back to trail leading into campground. Turn left at tne outhouses. The stake is visible from the edge of the ravine. To the left, there are 2 washes with a landmass in	35%BARE, 25% MXD Shrubs, 20% GRS, 10 % LEM, 10%CATT & stream veg. P
SR	SR017	LBSR17	PC	RIP	From 17, go back up to campground. Continue through campground and turn left just before you reach the last campsite on the left side. The stake is visible from the edge of t	25% GRS, 25% TOY/LEM, 10%CRK veg, 10%BACC, 15% SAGE, 10%HERBS, 5% BARE.
SR	SR018	LBSR18	PC	RIW		30%TOY,SCOAK,LEM, 15%GRS, 15% CRK veg, 15% HERBS, 10%SAGE, 10% BARE, 5% BACC.
SR	SR019	LBSR19	PC	RIH	SR19R at road.	85% GRS, 10% CRK veg, 5% BACC.
SR	SR020	LBSR20	PC	RIP		70%GRS, 20%BACC, 10% CRK veg.
SR	SR021	LBSR21	PC	RIP		70%GRS, 20%BACC, 10% CRK veg.
SR	SR022	LBSR22	PC	GRS		60%GRS, 35% BACC, 5%HERBS.
SR	SR023	LBSR23	PC	CSS	From SR22, stay to the left of the drainage.	75% SAGE/BACC, 20%GRS, 5% HERBS.
SR	SR024	LBSR24	PC	CSS	From SR23, the point is across a drainage and a ridge. It is 1/2 way down the other side of the ridge. Moderately strenuous.	80%BACC/SAGE, 15%GRS, 5% HERBS.
SR	SR025	LBSR25	PC	GRS	Point is about 25 m past the fence.	85% GRS, 10%HERBS, 5% BACC.
SR	SR026	LBSR26	PC	GRS	Point is located on top of the large rock shelter. Coming	55%GRS, 40%BACC/SAGE, 5% HERBS.
SR	SR027	LBSR27	PC	CSS	from SR26, the bottom of the canyon is wet, so it is necessary to walk up the side. The W side (opposite the shelter) is better most of the way. There	35%BACC/SAGE, 35% GRS, 25% ROCK, 5% HERBS.
SR	SR028	LBSR28	PC	CSS	Cross ditch to get to stake.	60%SAGE, 35%GRS, 5%HERBS.
SR	SR029	LBSR29	PC	CSS	Perpendicular to rd up ridge. Right above rocky area in sage.	60%GRS, 20%BACC, 15% SAGE, 5% HERBS.
SR	SR030	LBSR30	PC	CSS	Over ridge from SR 29.	50%GRS, 25%SAGE, 20%BACC, 5% HERBS.
SR	SR031	LBSR31	PC	CSS		80%GRS, 15% SAGE, 5% HERBS.

Island	Site Code	Site Name	Type	Habitat	Directions	Habitat Notes
SR	SR032	LBSR32	PC	CSS	From SR31, follow ravine game trail S and cross stream. Stake is near a Baccharis bush just above stream bank.	35%BACC, 30%SAGE, 30%GRS, 5% HERBS.
SR	SR033	LBSR33	PC	CSS	From SR32, go E along stream. Stake is about 30m up from stream.	50%SAGE, 30%BACC, 15%GRS, 5% HERBS.
SR	SR034	LBSR34	PC	GRS		65%GRS, 25%BARE, 5% BACC, 5% HERBS.
SR	SR035	LBSR35	PC	GRS	Looks back N into Bacc in drainage. 250m S of SR34.	50%BACC, 40%GRS, 10%HERBS.
SR	SR036	LBSR36	PC	GRS	Overlooking junction of two drainages.	95%GRS, 5%HERBS.
SR	SR037	LBSR37	PC	GRS	This point is very close to the road, so park the vehicle on the N side of the small hill just before the point. 37A is GPS'd as the parking place. There is a wide flat area to leave the vehicle.	80%low mixed herbs, 20%GRS.
SR	SR038	LBSR38	PC	GRS	From SR37, stay low on slope while traveling. Point is on the right side of the canyon. Along game trail at ledge with rock outcrop.	40% GRS, 25%BACC, 30%BARE, 5%HERBS. Wind protected.
SR	SR039	LBSR39	PC	GRS	Point lies over the next ridge from SR38, and on the opposite side of the stream. May want to cross stream as soon as possible. To get back to the road, go up to the top of the ridge and follow the ridgeline back.	90%GRS, 5% BARE, 5% HERBS.
SR	SR040	LBSR40	PC	CSS	33m W of road in thick Bacc/Sage.	90%BACC/SAGE, 5%GRS, 5% HERBS.
SR	SR041	LBSR41	PC	CSS		60%BACC/SAGE, 35%GRS, 5%HERBS.
SR	SR042	LBSR42	PC	CSS		65%SAGE, 20%BACC, 10%GRS, 5%HERBS.
SR	SR043	LBSR43	PC	CSS	Travel S down drainage and back up 250m.	80%SAGE, 15% BACC, 5% GRS, HERBS.
SR	SR044	LBSR44	PC	GRS		70%GRS, 25% BACC, 5%HERBS.
SR	SR045	LBSR45	PC	GRS		65%GRS, 25%BACC, 5%BARE, 5%HERBS.
SR	SR046	LBSR46	PC	GRS		45%GRS, 50%BACC, 5%HERBS.
SR	SR047	LBSR47	PC	GRS	Some riparian veg.	60%GRS, 40% BACC.
SR	SR048	LBSR48	PC	CHA		85%CHAP, 15% BARE
SR	SR049	LBSR49	PC	CSS	As road comes down into drainage valley, the point is on the left side on the hill.	35%GRS, 30%BACC, 30%SAGE, 5%HERBS.
SR	SR050	LBSR50	PC	GRS		95%GRS, 5%HERBS, occ. BACC.
SR	SR051	LBSR51	PC	CSS		40%GRS, 35%SAGE, 10%BARE, 10%HERBS, 5%BACC.

Island	Site Code	Site Name	Type	Habitat	Directions	Habitat Notes
SR	SR052	LBSR52	PC	CHA	Overlooking ravine facing SE. This transect is best run SR54-SR53-SR52, after doing the SR61-63 transect. Coming to SR52 from SR53, head down the drainage towards the road. Cut W before reaching the road.	40%CHAM, 30%SAGE, 25%SCROAK, 5%BARE.
SR	SR053	LBSR53	PC	GRS	From SR54, go up drainage at W end of the Torrey Pines. Point is approx 1/3 of the way up canyon on W bank.	65%GRS, 15%BARE, 10%SAGE, 10%HERBS.
SR	SR054	LBSR54	PC	GRS	Across road from SR63. Point is up E side of drainage.	90%GRS, 5%SCROAK, 5%HERBS.
SR	SR055	LBSR55	PC	CHA		40%CHAM, 40%SCROAK, 10%SMF(sticky monkey flower), 5% bare, 5% HERBS/GRS. SEE 2003 NOTES.
SR	SR056	LBSR56	PC	CSS	After leaving SR55, there will be a very tall stand of Bacc. Go to the left of the Bacc, over the grassy area, cross the ravine, then get back on track. Either go over the top of the hill, then way down the other	45%SCROAK, 25%ROCK, 20% SAGE, 10%BACC.
SR	SR057	LBSR57	PC	GRS	From SR56, follow game trail slightly W towards the stand of oaks. Turn E on the large game trail that parallels the ravine. Follow the trail until the ravine looks passable. The ravine has been wet in very dry years. Climb u	55%GRS, 40%BACC, 5%HERBS.
SR	SR058	LBSR58	PC	CHA	This transect is best run in reverse, SR60-SR59-SR58, after the SR55-57 transect. The hike from SR59 to SR58 is strenuous. Follow the drainage W, then as it turns NW until it begins to shallow out. Then climb up and over t	60%CHAM, 30%BARE, 10%SCROAK.
SR	SR059	LBSR59	PC	CSS	Very difficult to get to from either direction. SR60 lies directly over the S ridge. From SR60, head E around the ridge. Once around the ridge, head W up the drainage. There is a small game trail g	25%SCROAK, 20%BARE, 20%SAGE, 20%BACC, 10%GRS, 5%TOY. V
SR	SR060	LBSR60	PC	GRS	Coming from SR57, follow the game trail around the ridge to the E. The trail goes most of the way. It tapers off near a stand of oaks in a large drainage. Head S up the drainage, about 60m. Stake is in a rather	40%GRS, 35% BACC, 20%SCROAK, 5% HERBS.
SR	SR061	LBSR61	PC	CHA	Near Upper Torrey Pines rd. Walk down less steep ridge, then cross over to point. Or go down the drainage.	30%MANZ/OAK SCRUB, 30%CHAM, 25%GRS, 10% BARE, 5% SAGE/HERBS.
SR	SR062	LBSR62	PC	CHA	Come down drainage from SR61.	40%CHAM, 20%GRS, 20% MANZ/SCROAK, 15%BARE, 5%HERBS.
SR	SR063	LBSR63	PC	GRS	Continue down drainage from SR62. Point is across the lower road, about 4m from road.	95%GRS, 5%HERBS, occ BACC.
SR	SR064	LBSR64	PC	TOR		75%BARE, 20%TOR, 5%HERBS.

Island	Site Code	Site Name	Type	Habitat	Directions	Habitat Notes
SR	SR065	LBSR65	PC	TOR	Up stream bed, go over 2 steep ridges to the east. Stake is near small pine by game trail.	50%TOR, 30%GRS, 15%Pine needles, 5%BARE.
SR	SR066	LBSR66	PC	TOR	SW over 2 ridges.	35%TOR, 40%BARE, 20%MANZ, 5%SMF.
SR	SR067	LBSR67	PC	TOR	On ridge end overlooking junction of 2 drainages.	30%GRS, 25%TOR, 25%BARE, 15%SMF, 5% OAK SCRUB.
SR	SR068	LBSR68	PC	TOR		50%TOR, 30%GRS, 10%SCROAK, 5%BARE, 5%HERBS.
SR	SR069	LBSR69	PC	TOR		40%TOR, 40%Pine needles, 20%GRS.
SR	SR070	LBSR70	PC	CSS	On drainage facing NE.	35%GRS, 30%SAGE, 30%BACC. 5%HERBS.
SR	SR071	LBSR71	PC	CSS	Walk up ridge to W along canyon.	40%GRS, 30%SAGE, 20%BACC, 5%HERBS, 5%BARE.
SR	SR072	LBSR72	PC	GRS	Walk along drainage to top crossing.	85%GRS, 10%OAK scrub/TOR, 5%HERBS.
SR	SR073	LBSR73	PC	CHA	Off of Tel. Road.	50%CHAM, 45%SCROAK, 5%BARE.
SR	SR074	LBSR74	PC	CHA	Over ridge. WSW, between CCP and IO, on slope facing drainage.	60%OAK scrub, 20%GRS, 5%BACC, 5% CHAM, 5%HERBS, 5% SMF.
SR	SR075	LBSR75	PC	OAK	One ridge over from SR74.	25%IO, 25%CHAM, 20%GRS, 20%OAK scrub, 5%HERBS, 5% BARE.
SR	SR076	LBSR76	PC	CHA	Overlooking branched drainage.	30%SCROAK, 25%GRS, 15%BARE, 10%BACC, 10%HERBS, 10%SAGE.
SR	SR077	LBSR77	PC	CHA	From SR76, walk NNW over drainage up into scrub oak.	50%SCROAK, 25%BARE, 10%HERBS, 15%GRS.
SR	SR078	LBSR78	PC	CHA	From SR77, cross canyon to E following game trails to top of next ridge. Another option is to warlk around on ridge by the road.	55% SCROAK, 40%BARE, 5%GRS/HERBS.
SR	SR079	LBSR79	PC	MXW	Walk up ravine from road.	35%OAK, 25%GRS, 20%SAGE, 10%BACC, 10%BARE.
SR	SR080	LBSR80	PC	RIP		30%GRS, 20%BACC, 10% CTNWD, 10%HRSTL, 10%SAGE, 10% misc crk veg. 5% CATTAIL, 5% HERBS.
SR	SR081	LBSR81	PC	RIW	Above trail in rock clump.	25%WLLW, 25%GRS, 15%BARE, 15%BACC, 10%SAGE, 5% CRK VEG, 5%HERBS.
SR	SR082	LBSR82	PC	RIW	Below upper trail in sage.	30%SCROAK/WLLW, 25%SAGE, 15%BACC, 10%GRS 10% HERBS, 10%CRK VEG.

Island	Site Code	Site Name	Type	Habitat	Directions	Habitat Notes
SR	SR083	LBSR83	PC	RIW		30%OAK, 25%CRK VEG, 15%BACC, 10%BARE, 10%HERBS, 10%GRS.
SR	SR084	LBSR84	PC	RIH	ON E side of creek.	50%GRS, 20%BARE, 15% BACC, 10%CRK VEG, 5%HERBS.
SR	SR085	LBSR85	PC	RIP		25%BACC, 20%BARE, 20%GRS, 20%CRK VEG, 10%HERBS, 5%OAK.
SR	SR086	LBSR86	PC	CHA		40%OAK/TOY, 40%GRS, 10%BACC, 5%HERBS, 5% BARE.
SR	SR087	LBSR87	PC	CHA	From road, walk N over 2 ridges to the S. side of 3rd ridge along game trails.	60%SCROAK, 25%IO, 10%GRS, 5%HERBS.
SR	SR088	LBSR88	PC	OAK		95%IO, 5%GRS.
SR	SR089	LBSR89	PC	CHA		40% SCROAK, 35%GRS, 20%BACC, 5%HERBS.
SR	SR090	LBSR90	PC	OAK		90%IO, 10%GRS/BACC.
SR	SR091	LBSR91	PC	CCP		55%SCROAK/MANZ, 30%CCP, 15%BARE.
SR	SR092	LBSR92	PC	CCP	Walk on ridge from road (steep).	25%CCP, 25%BARE, 20%OAK, 15% HERBS, 15%GRS.
SR	SR093	LBSR93	PC	CCP		60%CCP, 30%BARE, 10%MANZ.
SR	SR094	LBSR94	PC	CCP	Walk S up ridge then drop down into pines near end of stand.	45%CCP, 30%BARE,15%GRS, 5%MANZ, 5%HERBS.
SR	SR095	LBSR95	PC	CHA	Walk across drainage to top of next ridge.	50%SCROAK, 45%CHAM, 5% BARE.
SR	SR096	LBSR96	PC	CHA	Walk up ridge then drop down into Manz. Cross small drainage and walk up next ridge to stake.	50%CHAM/MANZ, 30%SCROAK, 15%BARE.
SR	SR097	LBSR97	PC	CHA		90%SCROAK, 5%BARE, 5% SMFL.
SR	SR098	LBSR98	PC	CHA	Follow ridge down to site, heading toward housing.	80%SCROAK, 15%GRS, 5%HERBS.
SR	SR099	LBSR99	PC	CHA	From 98, Walk toward highest point to sight on SCI. Go down ridge through drainage and up next ridge to site.	45%CHAM, 30%SCROAK, 15%BARE, 5%HERBS, 5%MANZ(tiny).
SR	SR100	LBSR100	PC	OAK		
SR	SR101	LBSR101	PC	OAK		
SR	SR102	LBSR102	PC	OAK		
SR	SR103	LBSR103	PC	MXW		
SR	SR104	LBSR104	PC	CCP		
SR	SR105	LBSR105	PC	CCP		

Island	Site Code	Site Name	Type	Habitat	Directions	Habitat Notes
SR	SR106	LBSR106	PC	CHA		
SR	SR107	LBSR107	PC	CHA		
SR	SR108	LBSR108	PC	CHA		
SR	SR109	LBSR109	PC	CHA		
SR	SR110	LBSR110	PC	CHA		
SR	SR111	LBSR111	PC	CHA		
SR	SR112	LBSR112	PC	CHA		
SR	SR113	LBSR113	PC	CHA		
SR	SR114	LBSR114	PC	CHA		
SR	SR115	LBSR115	PC	CHA		
SR	SR116	LBSR116	PC	CSS		
SR	SR117	LBSR117	PC	CSS		
SR	SR118	LBSR118	PC	CSS		
SR	SR119	LBSR119	PC	CSS		
SR	SR120	LBSR120	PC	CSS		
SR	SR121	LBSR121	PC	CSS		
SR	SR122	LBSR122	PC	CSS		
SR	SR123	LBSR123	PC	CSS		
SR	SR124	LBSR124	PC	CSS		
SR	SR125	LBSR125	PC	CSS		
SR	SR126	LBSR126	PC	CSS		
SR	SR127	LBSR127	PC	CSS		
SR	SR128	LBSR128	PC	CSS		
SR	SR129	LBSR129	PC	CSS		
SR	SR130	LBSR130	PC	CSS		
SR	SR131	LBSR131	PC	MXW		
SR	SR132	LBSR132	PC	RIP		
SR	SR133	LBSR133	PC	RIH		
SR	SR134	LBSR134	PC	MXW		
SR	SR135	LBSR135	PC	RIP		
SR	SR136	LBSR136	PC	RIH		

Island	Site Code	Site Name	Type	Habitat	Directions	Habitat Notes
SR	SR137	LBSR137	PC	LUP		
SR	SR138	LBSR138	PC	LUP		
SR	SR139	LBSR139	PC	LUP		
SR	SR140	LBSR140	PC	LUP		
SR	SR141	LBSR141	PC	LUP		
SR	SR142	LBSR142	PC	MXW		
SR	SR143	LBSR143	PC	MXW		
SR	SR144	LBSR144	PC	MXW		
SR	SR145	LBSR145	PC	MXW		
SR	TP01	Torrey Pine 01	PC	TOR		
SR	TP02	Torrey Pine 02	PC	TOR		
SR	TP03	Torrey Pine 03	PC	TOR		
SR	TP04	Torrey Pine 04	PC	TOR		
SR	TP05	Torrey Pine 05	PC	TOR		
SR	TP06	Torrey Pine 06	PC	TOR		
SR	TP07	Torrey Pine 07	PC	TOR		
SR	TP08	Torrey Pine 08	PC	TOR		
SR	TP09	Torrey Pine 09	PC	TOR		
SR	TP10	Torrey Pine 10	PC	TOR		
SR	WD01	Woodland 01	PC	MXW		
SR	WD02	Woodland 02	PC	MXW		
SR	WD03	Woodland 03	PC	MXW		
SR	WD04	Woodland 04	PC	MXW		
SR	WD05	Woodland 05	PC	MXW		
SR	WD06	Woodland 06	PC	MXW		
SR	WD07	Woodland 07	PC	MXW		
SR	WD08	Woodland 08	PC	MXW		
SR	WD09	Woodland 09	PC	MXW		
SR	WD10	Woodland 10	PC	MXW		
SR	WD11	Woodland 11	PC	MXW		
SR	WD12	Woodland 12	PC	MXW		

Description of Legacy Line Transects Sampled 1993-2003

The following descriptions of the line transects that were sampled on East Anacapa, San Miguel, and Santa Barbara Islands between 1993 and 2003 are extracted from the 1988 Channel Islands National Park Monitoring Handbook (van Riper et al. 1988):

SANTA BARBARA ISLAND

Censuses on Santa Barbara Island are conducted from four trails and canyons. See Figure SOP 3-1. Orange-crowned Warblers are primarily found in the area of Cave, Middle, and Graveyard Canyons and counted there, while other breeding species are counted from the island trails.

Trails Used

Cave, Middle, and Graveyard Canyons: Cave, Middle, and Graveyard Canyons are the three canyons south of the residence area. The primary objective of the counts along the canyons is to determine the number of pairs of Orange-crowned Warblers, based on the singing males heard. Begin the count at official sunrise starting at the steps on the lower Landing Cove Trail. (Time of sunrise and sunset is announced periodically on Channel 1 - the weather station on the marine radio; it is also listed in tide tables.) Walk up from the Landing Cove, watching and listening for warblers, especially in the Coreopsis. At the top of the cove, proceed past the Quonset hut and follow the east side of the Nature Trail, again listening for singing warblers. At the southeast corner of the nature trail (i.e. above the mouth of Cave Canyon), walk slowly along the north rim of the canyon, listening and scanning the Coreopsis on the far side of the Canyon (be careful to avoid the nasty cholla which covers much of the north rim). When a warbler is heard, stop, note its location, and listen for other birds along the length of the canyon. Frequently you will be able to hear two males singing at once and hence be able to determine their relative locations; when you are along the middle stretch of the canyon, you will probably be able to locate all of the males along the entire length of the canyon. Be careful to avoid double-counting any of the singing males. Continue to the head of the canyon in this manner, then loop around the head of the canyon and walk down to the north side of the mouth of Middle Canyon (try to walk through grassy areas, avoiding the dense patches of boxthorn between the two canyons). From the mouth of Middle Canyon, slowly walk along the north rim toward the head of the canyon, listening for singing birds as described above.

From the head of Middle Canyon, walk to the bluff on the north side of Graveyard Canyon which overlooks the fork in the canyon. Walk west along the north rim on the old trail, then cross the north fork of the canyon to the north side of the south fork. Look and listen for warblers in the Coreopsis in the south fork. Finally, proceed to the large Coreopsis stand on the terrace north of the Badlands. Make a slow circuit around the periphery of this stand, again watching and listening for singing warblers. The entire count, from Landing Cove to the Coreopsis stand on the Badlands, should take about two hours.

Arch Point Loop: This trail begins at the residence area, goes up to the Saddle, turns north following the upper east slope of North Peak out to Arch Point, then returns to the residence area going through Cliff Canyon and around the head of the Landing Cove (note that this is the direction the trail should be walked - i.e. clockwise). Begin the census along this trail one hour after official sunrise.

Elephant Seat Cove Trail: Begin this trail at sunrise. Start at the Saddle and follow the trail down onto the west terrace and across Webster Point. End the count at the Elephant Seal overlook. Return to the Saddle. Signal Peak loop may be done immediately following.

Signal Peak Loop: Begin this trail at the Saddle, and proceed up to the top of Signal Peak (also walk out to the end of the overlook spur which branches off to the right just after you reach the top of the peak). From the top of the peak, follow the trail down the east slope, through Cat Canyon, along the top of the Southeast Rookery slope, and across the Badlands. End the count at the "Y" where the Signal Peak Trail runs into the Saddle Trail. Begin this count one hour after official sunrise.

Time of Each Count

Cave, Middle, and Graveyard Canyons
    Begin at sunrise
    Walk rim of canyons—1 ¾ to 2 hours

Arch Point Loop
    Begin one hour after sunrise
    Walk loop—1 to 1 ½ hours

Elephant Seal Cove Trail
    Begin at sunrise
    Saddle to Elephant Seal Cove and back—45 minutes

Signal Peak Loop
    Begin one hour after sunrise
    Walk trail—1 to 1 ½ hours

East Anacapa Island

Census is limited to East Anacapa Island because of access difficulties and potential disturbance of the endangered California Brown Pelican on West Anacapa Island. See Figure SOP 3-2. The entire island is surveyed in one day using two major trails.

Trail Used

The East Anacapa Island census starts at the gate to the lighthouse, with the observer slowly walking to the ranger residence. At the bunkhouse, turn upslope and travel around the helicopter pad, proceeding down toward the campground and turning left at that trail junction. Continue along this trail, staying to the left at the fork, until you reach the western tip of the island (Inspiration Point). Turn here and follow the north loop of this trail down through the gull colony. Retrace the path to the campground (do not recount the section of trail you already covered), then turn left (north) and follow the Cathedral Cove trail. Where the Cathedral Cove trail meets the main trail, turn left and walk back to the residence area ending the count at the bunkhouse.

Time of Each Count

Begin at dawn
Walk trail—1 to 1 ½ hours

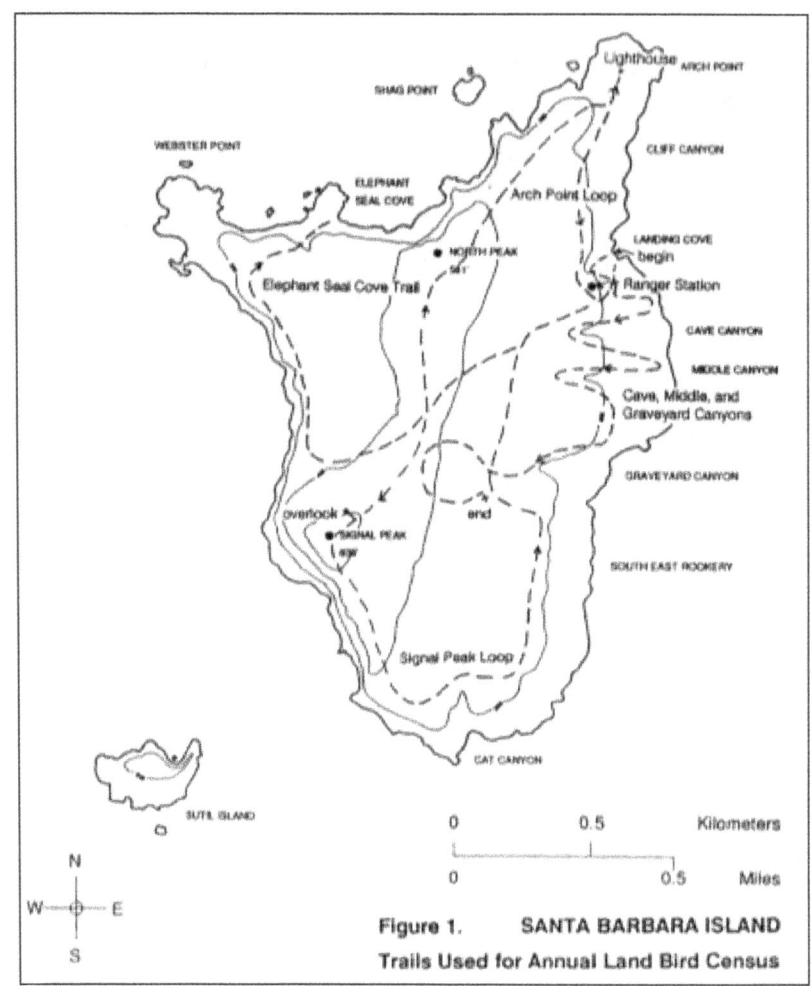

Figure SOP 3-1. Location of legacy line transect surveys on Santa Barbara Island.

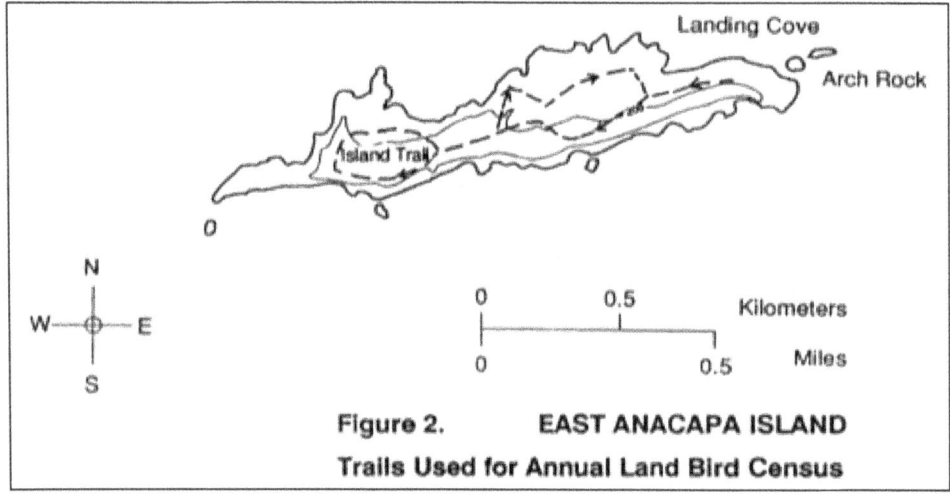

Figure SOP 3-2. Locations of legacy line transect surveys on East Anacapa Island.

SAN MIGUEL ISLAND

Trails Used

There are three basic trail systems used for counts on San Miguel Island. They are described here and mapped in Figure SOP 3-3.

Cross-Island Trail: Begin at the Nidever Creek Bridge between the ranger station and the outhouse. Follow the trail, turning right at the junction to the Cabrillo Monument (do not take the small loop up to the actual monument) and on to San Miguel Hill (end day one).

On day two, continue over San Miguel Hill and Green Mountain, down the west slope of Green Mountain, and through the large section of lupine which ends just before the dry lake bed. The end of this lupine patch marks the end of the count.

Harris Point Administrative Trail: A marker indicates the beginning of this route, where the Harris Point administrative trail joins the old jeep trail. Follow the trail north approximately 1600 m to markers that indicate the end of the count

Willow Canyon: Although not technically a trail, the bottom of Willow Canyon is easily traveled and presents a good route for monitoring unique canyon habitats. Begin censusing at the north western most extension of upper Willow Canyon, approximately 50 m north of where the old fence line crosses the canyon. Follow the bottom of the canyon all the way to the mouth (Willow Cove). Keep to the main canyon, staying to the left at all major junctions.

Time of Each Count

Cross-Island Trail (census over two days):
Begin at dawn
Time to San Miguel Hill—2 hours
Time to end of count—4 ½ hours
Transit time back to ranger station—2 ½ to 3 hours

Harris Point Trail
Begin at dawn
Transit time to beginning of count—20 minutes
Count time—50 minutes
Transit time back to ranger station—45 minutes

Willow Canyon
Begin at dawn
Transit time to beginning of count—20 minutes
Count time—2 ½ hours
Transit time back to ranger station—1 ½ to 2 hours

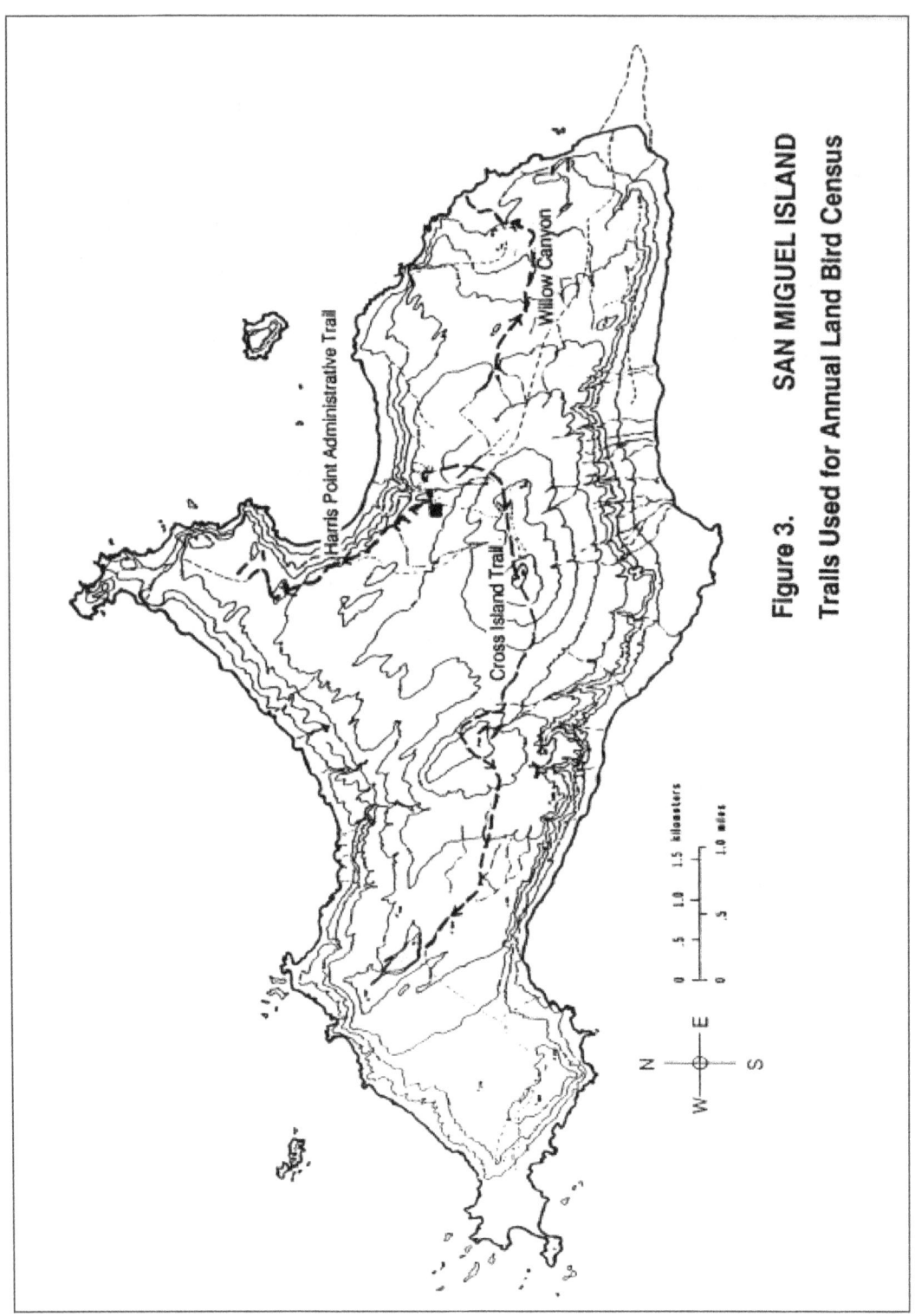

Figure SOP 3-3. Locations of legacy line transect surveys on San Miguel Island.

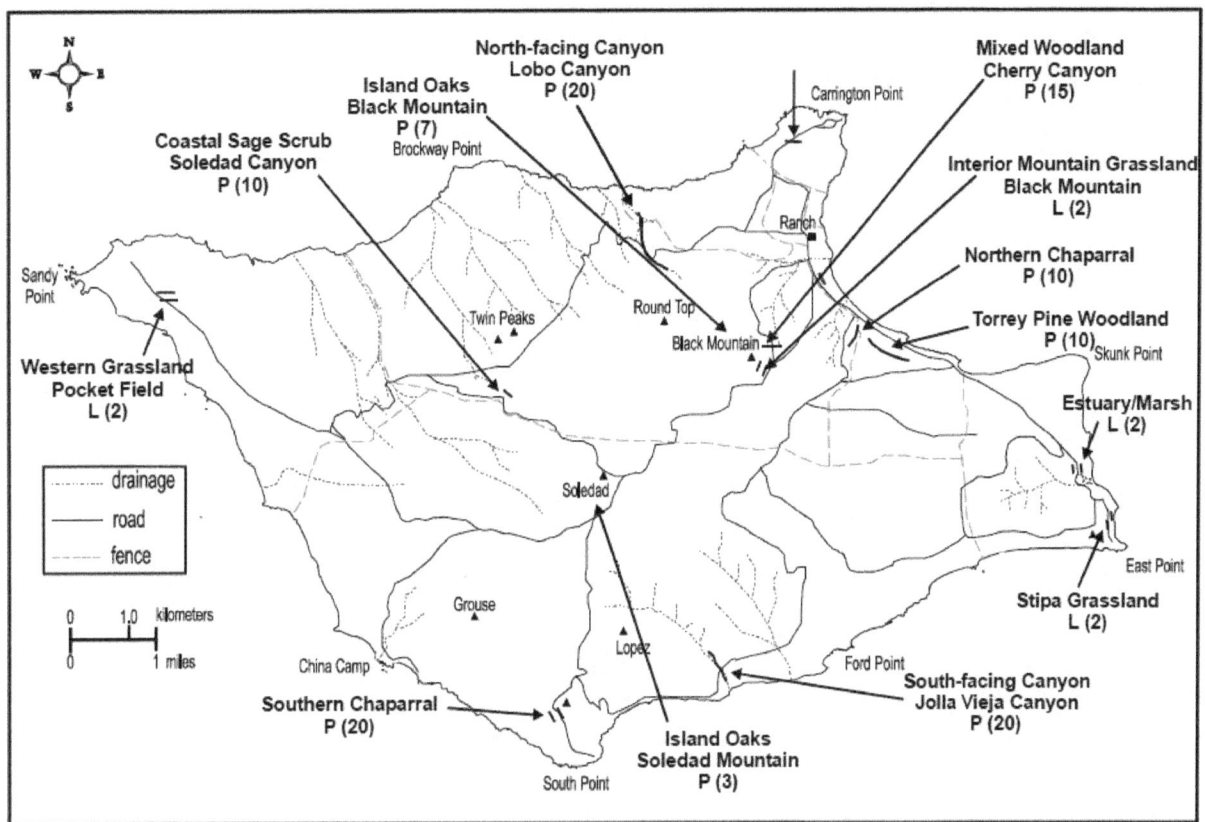

Figure SOP 3-4. Locations of legacy line transect and point count monitoring sites on Santa Rosa Island. (L = line transect, P = cluster of point-count stations).

Standard Operating Procedure (SOP) # 4

Photographic Documentation of Landbird Monitoring Sites
Version 1.00 (2011)

Revision History Log:

Prev. Version #	Revision Date	Author	Changes Made	Reason for Change	New Version #

The purpose of this Standard Operating Procedure (SOP) is to provide photo documentation of the landbird monitoring sites. Ideally this will be done once initially with the implementation of the program revision and then once every 5 years.

Camera settings:

1. Photo size setting may be at any size, but the ideal settings are at about 1280x960 or 1600x1200 with normal resolution or approximately 3-5MP. This will create an image that is a reasonable size to archive.
2. Do not zoom in. Set lens at widest angle possible.
3. Auto focus and auto shutter may be used. Set auto shutter to expose the terrain, not the sky.
4. Since the use of digital cameras allows for reuse of storage, taking multiple pictures from each position is possible if needed to get good photos. It is better to take more photos while onsite than regret not doing so when back in the office.
5. Ideal conditions: Clear day, sun high in sky, (2 hrs. after sunrise to 2 hrs. before sunset).

Methodology:

1. Start by taking a photo of the GPS face showing the site and its coordinates and other pertinent information at the site stake. This photo will be used in the protocol appendix to help find the site.
2. Stand at the stake and use the GPS to take the photos, taking one photo in each of the cardinal directions (N, S, and E, W).
3. Begin at the North cardinal direction.
4. Take picture in landscape orientation (not portrait).
5. Take the photo as level (both vertically and horizontally) as possible, and focus to expose the terrain, not capturing much of the sky.
6. Note your location relative to the station (the following sheet can be used for this purpose). Items that can be noted here include the photo sequence, or the start position.
7. Go to the next position, checking your orientation, and repeat.
8. Repeat the steps until site photographs have been taken in all four cardinal directions.
9. Now walk away from the site stake in the direction from which you would enter the site and take a photograph. Make every effort to ensure that the site stake is still visible in the center of the photo and not hidden.

Additional photographs: Take a few photos in a good location to capture the whole scene, several hundred feet to a quarter mile from the monitoring site.. Additional photographs may be taken that show any element of interest that might not have been captured in the sequence. These may include photos from a greater distance that illustrate the station exposure.

Photo Names: LB*IslandSite#Direction date*.jpg.
LB – Landbird Program, 2 letter island code, LB site number, date (M DD YY); jpg format.
Store the photos at this location on the U Drive, RM Server:
U:\NRM\IM\LandBird\LBMonPhotos*Island\Filename**

Movie clips: Many new digital cameras are capable of taking short streaming video or .avi format video clips. A short (45-70 sec. duration) video clip can be taken to give a 360 degree (panoramic) sweep of the site setting. To do this, start at the site stake and begin by aiming due north, begin the .avi exposure and slowly rotate in a clockwise direction until again aiming north, pause briefly (~1 sec.) then stop the exposure. You may also want to take a video file of the site area as you walk into the site. Select a location in proximity to the station (usually 100 to 200 feet away). Typically, this location would be at an elevated vantage point relative to the station. Start to your left and begin the .avi exposure and slowly rotate in a clockwise direction approximately 180 degrees, pause briefly (~1 sec.) then stop the exposure.

Required tools:
1. Camera
2. Extra Batteries for camera or means to recharge
3. Computer to download pictures from camera
4. Sunshade (Hat with brim) to view camera LCD.

Photo Data to Include: (* is required; other fields are standard as completed below)
Park Code CHIS
Network Code MEDN
Program: LB
Photo Name _____ *
Date: _____ *
Photographer: _____ *
Description: _____ *
UTM East: _____ *
UTM North: _____ *
Datum: _____ *
Network Folder Archive U:\NRM\IM\LandBird\LBMonPhotos*Island\Filename**
Photo Format .JPG
Rights: Public
Collection: CHIS/MEDN
Publisher NPS
Resource Type: Image

Conducting Point Count Surveys
Version 1.00 (2011)

Revision History Log:

Prev. Version #	Revision Date	Author	Changes Made	Reason for Change	New Version #

This Standard Operating Procedure (SOP) gives step-by-step instructions for conducting point count surveys to monitor landbirds at Channel Islands National Park using the Variable Circular Plot (VCP) distance-sampling methodology. The SOP describes the procedure for collecting data and filling in the "CHIS Landbird Surveys" data form (Figure SOP 5-1).

Procedures:

1. Prior to the day of the counts, determine which plots will be sampled and in which order, and make certain that the UTM coordinates for those points are in the GPS unit. As a backup, bring a list of UTM coordinates for each point. If necessary, UTM coordinates can be entered manually.

2. Wear earth-tone colors (browns, greens, dark blues, grays). Do not wear bright colors (reds, yellows, whites, etc.).

3. The point counts should only be conducted if conditions meet the following criteria:
    *   Visibility is greater than 400 m.
    *   Wind is 10 knots or less (i.e., less than 4 on the Beaufort scale).
    *   It is not raining heavily.
    *   No one has walked or driven through the area to be counted within 30 minutes prior to the count.
    *   Only one observer is within the count circle (no additional persons may accompany the observer).
    *   The landbird survey must be the first priority. If anything else is done in addition (e.g., transporting some materials), it must not in any way detract from the time and attention you are giving the survey, nor should it affect the pace at which you cover the survey route.

4. Sampling will occur in the morning, beginning as soon as it is light enough to see a distance of at least 400 m and ending no later than 4 hours after official sunrise. Try to arrive at the

first plot while it is still dark so that the count can begin as soon as it is light enough to see. Singing rate for most species is usually highest before or near official sunrise and then declines slowly for the next four hours.

5. Do not conduct the count during high winds or heavy rains because these conditions inhibit bird activity and impair your ability to see and hear birds. Counts should not be conducted if wind strength on the Beaufort Scale is a sustained 4 or greater (see Table SOP 5-1), or if it is raining hard or snowing (rain code ≥ 4 in Table SOP 5-2). If you encounter these conditions, wait until the weather improves or else cancel the sampling for today and try again on another day.

6. Navigate to the coordinates of the next plot on the list using the GPS. If the hike to the point was extremely strenuous, rest away from the point (e.g., 100 m) for a few minutes, then continue to the point. At the first point on each survey day, fill in the survey information at the top of the form. At the first and last survey points, fill in the survey condition data.

7. Conduct the point as a "snapshot" in time. The survey results should represent the actual distribution of the birds relative to the point. The underlying theory of distance sampling requires that each point be recorded as close to a "snapshot in time" as possible. Some movement is acceptable, as long as a bird is only counted once and the observer does not cause movement. Any birds that flush upon approaching the point, or birds that seem to be attracted by the presence of the surveyors, should be noted in the comments.

8. Use a laser rangefinder to estimate distances to birds whenever possible; the closer the bird, the more accurate the distance estimation should be.

9. Remember: **The goal is not the largest count possible, but the most accurate count possible. Stick to the methodology described in this protocol.** Do not bend the rules to include more birds because you think that you do not have enough. Do not list a bird unless you are sure of its identification. The accuracy and integrity of the count can only be maintained by minimizing variations in methodology. This is accomplished by rigorously following the established count procedures.

10. The accuracy and integrity of the count can only be maintained by minimizing variations in methodology. This is accomplished by rigorously following the established count procedures.

Completing the top portion of the "CHIS Landbird Surveys" Form

Island: Enter the 2-character island code: AN (East Anacapa), SB (Santa Barbara), SC (Santa Cruz), SM (San Miguel), SR (Santa Rosa).

Site Code: Unique identifier for the point count station or the line transect (see SOP # 3 for list of site codes).

LT or PC: Circle PC since this is a point count station.

Date (mm/dd/yyyy): Write in the month (2 digits), day (2 digits) and year (4 digits) in the format shown. Examples are 05/02/2011 and 06/25/2011.

Observer initials: Fill in the three initials of the person conducting the counts using capital letters. If you do not have a middle name, then put an underscore for your middle initial.

Start Time (hh:mm): Write in the hour and minute when you began the line transect count or the 10-minute point count. Use military time format for times after noon (e.g., 13:05, 14:26).

Weather conditions during the survey:
The following information should be filled in at the beginning or end of each 10-minute count whenever possible.

Temp(erature) (°C): Record the ambient temperature during the ten-minute count in degrees Celsius, rounded off to the nearest degree. The thermometer should be placed above the ground and allowed to adjust to ambient air temperature.

Wind (0–6): Record the wind code (0 through 6; Table 5.01.2) as it applies to the strength of the wind during the count. Record the average wind conditions for each count, not the maximum condition (e.g., periods of gusty winds).

Table SOP 5-1. Codes (Beaufort scale) used to record wind strength during bird counts.

Wind Code	Definition
0	calm, smoke rises vertically (< 2 km/h)
1	smoke drifts (2-5 km/h)
2	light breeze felt on face, leaves rustle (6-12 km/h)
3	leaves and twigs in constant motion (13-19 km/h)
4	small branches move, raises loose paper, dust rises (20-29 km/h)
5	fresh breeze, small trees sway (30-39 km/h)
6	strong breeze, large branches moving, wind whistling (40-50 km/h)

Precip(itation) **(0–5): Record the appropriate code (Table SOP 5-2).**

Table SOP 5-2. Codes used to record precipitation during bird counts.

Rain Code	Definition
0	no rain
1	mist or fog
2	light drizzle
3	light rain
4	heavy rain; difficult to hear birds (stop the count)
5	Snow (stop the count)

Clouds (%): Visual estimate of the percent cloud cover, rounded off to the nearest 10%. This should be a number between 0 (no clouds) and 100 (completely overcast). If there are patches of clouds in different areas of the sky, try to picture gathering all of them together into one part of the sky and record what percent of cloud cover that would represent. If you are in thick fog, record 100%, even if it is a bright sunny day up above the fog layer that you are conducting the count in.

Noise (0–3): Record the noise code (Table SOP 5-3) that applies to background-noise conditions during the count, as it affects your ability to hear birds.

Table SOP 5-3. Codes used to record level of background noise as it affects the observer's ability to hear birds.

Noise Code	Definition
0	quiet; normal background noises; no interference
1	low noise; might be missing some high-pitched songs/calls of distant birds
2	medium noise; detection radius is probably substantially reduced
3	high noise; probably detecting only the loudest/closest birds

Approaching the Point and Beginning the Count

11. Approach the plot vigilantly, and if you observe a bird close to the center of the plot that flushes as a result of you approaching the plot, you should record the initial distance from the plot center to that bird on the data form. The reason for this is that a critical assumption of the distance methodology is that any bird directly at (or very close to, e.g., <5-10 m) the plot center will always be detected, i.e., $g(0) = 1$. If the data are analyzed as grouped data (as recommended), this is not a problem if the bird does not move beyond the first grouping interval. However, if a bird that otherwise would have been recorded in the plot during the count flushes prior to the beginning of the count as a result of the approach of the observer, abundance will be underestimated for that species. The alternative approach is to wait for several minutes after reaching the plot before starting the count, but this approach is likely to underestimate bird density near the plot because of birds flushing as the observer approaches.

12. Once you arrive at the plot center, begin the count as soon as possible. You should have time to fill in the location, event, and weather conditions information at the top of the form during the count. If not, these can be filled in at the end of the 10-minute count.

13. Use a digital watch with a timer set at ten (10) minutes. Begin the survey by starting the timer at the top of a minute (zero seconds) so that you can record the time (hh:mm) and later determine whether each detection occurred during the first three minutes of the count, first five minutes, or during minutes 5-10. Stop the count at the end of the tenth minute.

14. Conduct the 10-minute count without interruption, being sure to fill in all the fields for each bird/flock detected. Occasionally, aircraft noise can be loud and can last for up to 30 seconds. In these instances, increase the count period by the amount of time for which the count was disturbed. If excessive noise interrupts the count for more than two minutes, then start the survey again after the disturbance has passed.

15. Once you have started your watch and begun the 10-minute counting period, record all birds heard or seen during the ten minutes, regardless of their distance from the center of the point. At each point, you will record the following information only once:

The following information will be recorded for each bird or flock of birds observed during the 10-minute active period:

- **Time** (hh:mm): Write in the hour and minute in which the bird was detected. Use military time format for times after noon (e.g., 13:05, 14:26).

- **Species**: Record the four-character code for the species detected. Examples are WEME for Western Meadowlark, HOLA for Horned Lark, and WIWA for Wilson's Warbler. Codes for species known to occur at Channel Islands NP are listed in Appendix A of this protocol. If no birds are detected during the ten-minute count, you should enter data for the first line of the form and record the code "NONE" in the Species column. Birds that you cannot positively identify to species should be recorded as "UNKN" for unknown bird (you may be able to identify it later during the 10-min count, and you will have the proper time of detection recorded for it).

- **Dist**(ance) (m): Record the horizontal distance in meters between the point center (where you are standing), and the location of the bird where you first detect it. Use a laser rangefinder whenever possible to get as accurate a distance as possible. **Do not round off numbers to the nearest five meters; estimate the distance to the nearest meter**. Many birds are heard and not seen. If you cannot see the bird, estimate the distance to some object (tree, bush, rock) near where you think the bird is located. If the bird is flying directly at you and then lands nearby, record the distance to where you first saw it flying toward you, not the distance to where it landed. For species that occur in clusters or flocks, record the distance from the observer to the center of the flock. If a bird is high in a tree, imagine dropping a plumb bob from the bird down to the ground, and measure the horizontal distance to that spot on the ground. Indicate flyovers (birds that fly above the top of the vegetation canopy, never touch down in your field of view, and do not appear to be foraging, displaying, or behaving in any other way that might suggest a link to the habitat below them) by entering -9999 in the distance column.

- **DT** (Detection type): The detection type corresponds to the first detection of that individual. The three possible entries for the first detection are "C" for Call, "S" for Song, and "V" for Visual. If you hear the bird and then later see it, add a "V" to the right of the "C" or "S" that you initially recorded, so that the Detection Type becomes "CV" or "SV". The detection type code will be used later in various analyses. For example, distances to birds that are seen are probably more accurate than those to birds that are only heard. Recording the detection type makes it possible to develop distance histograms to compare birds seen versus those that are only heard.

- **Flock Size**: For most observations, each individual bird will be treated independently as a separate observation with a Flock Size of one (1), but for species that usually occur in clusters or flocks, the appropriate unit is the cluster or flock size, and not the individual bird. For example, if you observe a flock of 15 House Finches moving as a group during a count, it is not appropriate to record 15 distances and treat them as independent observations in the analysis. For flocking species, record the distance to the center of the flock and the number of birds in the flock, rather than the distance to each individual bird.

- **Sex**: If you are able to see a sexually dimorphic species, record either "M" (male) or "F" (female) on the form; otherwise, leave blank. Leave the "sex" field blank for all auditory detections and for flocks that contain both males and females.

- **Age** (Class): If you are able to determine that a bird is a juvenile based on its plumage or vocalization, enter a "J" for Juvenile; otherwise, leave blank.

- **Prev**(ious) **Point**: Place an "X" in this column if the bird was already detected at a previous point. Bias caused by repeated counting of the same individual from more than one point is usually small unless repeated counting is common during a survey (Buckland et al. 2001:37) or in cases where a rare bird is counted from multiple points (Nelson and Fancy 1999). By recording whether a bird is thought to have been counted at a previous point, the data can later be analyzed in two different ways, depending on which is most appropriate. Some authorities say that you should not count a bird if you think it was already recorded from another point. Others argue that you should always count each bird detected, even if it was probably detected previously. By placing an "X" in this column for those cases in which you think the bird has already been counted from another point, you allow future investigators the option of analyzing data using either approach.

- **Comments**: Record any comments that seem appropriate and that might help someone interpret and analyze the data correctly.

After the 10-minute Active Period

16. Review the data form and fill in all fields on the data form before departing for the next point. Also, search the area to ensure that no equipment is left behind.

17. Record observations of other notable plant and animal species on the separate "Incidental Observations" data form (Figure SOP 5-2).

Literature Cited:

Buckland, S. T., D. R. Anderson, K. P. Burnham, J. L. Laake, D. L. Borchers, and L. Thomas. 2001. Introduction to distance sampling: Estimating abundance of biological populations. Oxford, U.K.: Oxford University Press.

Nelson, J. T., and S. G. Fancy. 1999. A test of the variable circular-plot method where exact density of a bird population was known. Pacific Conservation Biology 5:139–143.

CHIS Landbird Surveys

Island: ___ Site Code: _____ **LT PC** Date (mm/dd/yyyy): _____ Observer: ____

Conditions: Temp. (C): ___ Wind (0-6): ___ Precip (0-5): ___ Clouds (0-100): ___ Noise (0-3): ___ Start Time (hh:mm): ___

Time	Species	Dist. (m)	DT	Flock Size	Sex	Age	Prev. Point	Comments

Island: ___ Site Code: _____ **LT PC** Date (mm/dd/yyyy): _____ Observer: ____

Conditions: Temp. (C): ___ Wind (0-6): ___ Precip (0-5): ___ Clouds (0-100): ___ Noise (0-3): ___ Start Time (hh:mm): ___

Time	Species	Dist. (m)	DT	Flock Size	Sex	Age	Prev. Point	Comments

CHIS Landbird Surveys

Island: ____ Site Code: _____ **LT PC** Date (mm/dd/yyyy): _____ Observer: ____

Conditions: Temp. (C): ___ Wind (0-6): __ Precip (0-5): __ Clouds (0-100): ___ Noise (0-3): ___ Start Time (hh:mm): _____

Time	Species	Dist. (m)	DT	Flock Size	Sex	Age	Prev. Point	Comments

Standard Operating Procedure (SOP) # 6

Conducting Line Transect Surveys
Version 1.00 (2011)

Revision History Log:

Prev. Version #	Revision Date	Author	Changes Made	Reason for Change	New Version #

This Standard Operating Procedure (SOP) gives step-by-step instructions for conducting line transect surveys to monitor landbirds at Channel Islands National Park using distance-sampling methodology. The SOP describes the procedure for collecting data and filling in the "CHIS Landbird Surveys" data form (Figure SOP 5-1).

Procedures:

1. Prior to the day of the counts, determine which transects will be sampled and in which order, and make certain that the UTM coordinates for those transects are in the GPS unit. As a backup, bring a list of UTM coordinates for each waypoint. If necessary, UTM coordinates can be entered manually.

2. Wear earth-tone colors (browns, greens, dark blues, grays). Do not wear bright colors (reds, yellows, whites, etc.).

3. The line transect can only be conducted if conditions meet the following criteria:
   - Visibility is greater than 400 m.
   - Wind is 10 knots or less (i.e., less than 4 on the Beaufort scale).
   - It is not raining heavily.
   - No one has walked the trail within 30 minutes prior to the count.
   - Only one observer conducts each transect survey (no additional persons may accompany the observer).
   - The landbird survey must be the first priority. If anything else is done in addition (e.g., transporting some materials), it must not in any way detract from the time and attention you are giving the survey, nor should it affect the pace at which you cover the survey route.

4. Sampling will occur in the morning, beginning as soon as it is light enough to see a distance of at least 400 m and ending no later than 4 hours after official sunrise. Try to

arrive at the start of the transect while it is still dark so that the count can begin as soon as it is light enough to see. Singing rate for most species is usually highest before or near official sunrise and then declines slowly for the next four hours.

5. Do not conduct the count during high winds or heavy rains because these conditions inhibit bird activity and impair your ability to see and hear birds. Counts should not be conducted if wind strength on the Beaufort Scale is a sustained 4 or greater (see Table SOP 6-1), or if it is raining hard or snowing (rain code $\geq$4 in Table SOP 6-2). If you encounter these conditions, wait until the weather improves or else cancel the sampling for today and try again on another day.

6. Navigate to the start of the transect using the GPS. If the hike to the point was extremely strenuous, rest away from the transect starting point (e.g., 100 m) for a few minutes, then continue to the point. Fill in the survey information at the top of the form, including the weather and other survey condition data.

7. Use a laser rangefinder to estimate the perpendicular distance between the transect and the birds whenever possible. The closer the bird is to the transect, the more accurate the distance estimation should be.

8. Remember: **The goal is not the largest count possible, but the most accurate count possible. Stick to the methodology described in this protocol.** Do not bend the rules to include more birds because you think that you do not have enough. Do not list a bird unless you are sure of its identification. The accuracy and integrity of the count can only be maintained by minimizing variations in methodology. This is accomplished by rigorously following the established count procedures.

9. The accuracy and integrity of the count can only be maintained by minimizing variations in methodology. This is accomplished by rigorously following the established count procedures.

Completing the top portion of the "CHIS Landbird Surveys" Form

Island: Enter the 2-character island code: AN (East Anacapa), SB (Santa Barbara), SC (Santa Cruz), SM (San Miguel), SR (Santa Rosa).

Site Code: Unique identifier for the line transect (see SOP # 3 for list of site codes).

LT or PC: Circle LT since this is a line transect.

Date (mm/dd/yyyy): Write in the month (2 digits), day (2 digits) and year (4 digits) in the format shown. Examples are 05/02/2011 and 06/25/2011.

Observer initials: Fill in the three initials of the person conducting the count using capital letters. If you do not have a middle name, then put an underscore for your middle initial.

Start Time (hh:mm): Write in the hour and minute when you began the line transect count. Use military time format for times after noon (e.g., 13:05, 14:26).

Weather conditions during the survey:

Temp(erature) (°C): Record the ambient temperature in degrees Celsius, rounded off to the nearest degree. The thermometer should be placed above the ground and allowed to adjust to ambient air temperature.

Wind (0–6): Record the wind code (0 through 6; Table SOP 6-1) as it applies to the strength of the wind during the survey. Record the average wind conditions over the duration of the line transect survey, not the maximum condition (e.g., periods of gusty winds).

Table SOP 6-1. Codes (Beaufort scale) used to record wind strength during bird counts.

Wind Code	Definition
0	calm, smoke rises vertically (< 2 km/h)
1	smoke drifts (2-5 km/h)
2	light breeze felt on face, leaves rustle (6-12 km/h)
3	leaves and twigs in constant motion (13-19 km/h)
4	small branches move, raises loose paper, dust rises (20-29 km/h)
5	fresh breeze, small trees sway (30-39 km/h)
6	strong breeze, large branches moving, wind whistling (40-50 km/h)

Precip(itation) (0–5): Record the appropriate code from Table SOP 6-2.

Table SOP 6-2. Codes used to record precipitation during bird counts.

Rain Code	Definition
0	no rain
1	mist or fog
2	light drizzle
3	light rain
4	heavy rain; difficult to hear birds (stop the count)
5	snow (stop the count)

Clouds (%): Visual estimate of the percent cloud cover, rounded off to the nearest 10%. This should be a number between 0 (no clouds) and 100 (completely overcast). If there are patches of clouds in different areas of the sky, try to picture gathering all of them together into one part of the sky and record what percent of cloud cover that would represent. If you are in thick fog, record 100%, even if it is a bright sunny day up above the fog layer that you are conducting the count in.

Noise (0–3): Record the noise code (Table SOP 6-3) that applies to background-noise conditions during the duration of the transect, as it affects your ability to hear birds.

Table SOP 6-3. Codes used to record level of background noise as it affects the observer's ability to hear birds.

Noise Code	Definition
0	quiet; normal background noises; no interference
1	low noise; might be missing some high-pitched songs/calls of distant birds
2	medium noise; detection radius is probably substantially reduced
3	high noise; probably detecting only the loudest/closest birds

Conducting the Line Transect Survey

10. The observer will walk pre-designated routes and estimate the distance between the transect midline and the bird for all birds seen or heard (routes are identified for each island). Walk each trail at a moderately slow, steady pace. Consecutive counts on the same trail should all take about the same amount of time. Pause only to confirm identification of a bird.

11. Record all sightings of breeding species seen or heard on either side of the trail. Record the perpendicular distance from the transect midline to the birds in meters. Estimate the distance to the bird to the nearest meter (for example, record the distance as 43 m rather than rounding off to the nearest 5 m). Record whether the bird was first detected by its call, song, or visually. Count only those birds detected in the area directly to the sides of or in front of the observer. Do not count birds detected behind the observer.

12. Avoid counting the same bird more than once. For example, if you see a bird fly into a bush ahead of you, list it. As you approach the bush and pass by it, one bird of the same species flies out. It is reasonable to assume this is the same bird, so you would not count it as a sighting when it flew out of the bush. However, unless you can be reasonably certain that you have already counted a particular individual bird (as in this example), consider it a separate sighting.

13. Birds may be counted if they are on the ground, in vegetation, or in flight. Flying birds may be counted at any height.

14. Birds may be detected aurally if call notes or song are clearly heard and recognized. Many songs can be heard from great distances, so try to visually locate the singing bird to accurately determine the distance. If the bird cannot be seen, do your best to estimate the distance and list it as an observation. If you cannot make a reasonable distance estimate, do not count it. Use of laser range finders can greatly assist in distance estimation.

The following information will be recorded on the CHIS Landbird Surveys form for each bird or flock of birds observed along the line transect route:

• **Time** (hh:mm): Write in the hour and minute in which the bird was detected. Use military time format for times after noon (e.g., 13:05, 14:26).

• **Species**: Record the four-character code for the species detected. Examples are WEME for Western Meadowlark, HOLA for Horned Lark, and WIWA for Wilson's Warbler. Codes for species known to occur at Channel Islands NP are listed in Appendix A of this protocol. If you don't detect any birds at all for the transect (this is very unlikely), you should enter the code "NONE" in the Species column as the first record. Birds that you cannot positively identify to species should be recorded as "UNKN" for unknown bird (you may be able to identify it later, and you will have the proper time of detection recorded for it).

- **Dist**(ance) (m): Record the horizontal distance in meters between the midline of the transect and the location of the bird where you first detect it. Use a laser rangefinder whenever possible to get as accurate a distance as possible. **Do not round off numbers to the nearest five meters; estimate the distance to the nearest meter**. Many birds are heard and not seen. If you cannot see the bird, estimate the distance to some object (tree, bush, rock) near where you think the bird is located. If the bird is flying directly at you and then lands nearby, record the distance from the transect midline to where you first saw it flying toward you, not the distance to where it landed. For species that occur in clusters or flocks, record the distance from the transect midline to the center of the flock. If a bird is high in a tree, imagine dropping a plumb bob from the bird down to the ground, and measure the horizontal distance to that spot on the ground. Indicate flyovers (birds that fly above the top of the vegetation canopy, never touch down in your field of view, and do not appear to be foraging, displaying, or behaving in any other way that might suggest a link to the habitat below them) by entering -9999 in the distance column.

- **DT** (Detection type): The detection type corresponds to the first detection of that individual. The three possible entries for the first detection are "C" for Call, "S" for Song, and "V" for Visual. If you hear the bird and then later see it, add a "V" to the right of the "C" or "S" that you initially recorded, so that the Detection Type becomes "CV" or "SV". The detection type code will be used later in various analyses. For example, distances to birds that are seen are probably more accurate than those to birds that are only heard. Recording the detection type makes it possible to develop distance histograms to compare birds seen versus those that are only heard.

- **Flock Size**: For most observations, each individual bird will be treated independently as a separate observation with a Flock Size of one (1), but for species that usually occur in clusters or flocks, the appropriate unit is the cluster or flock size, and not the individual bird. For example, if you observe a flock of 15 House Finches moving as a group during a count, it is not appropriate to record 15 distances and treat them as independent observations in the analysis. For flocking species, record the distance to the center of the flock and the number of birds in the flock, rather than the distance to each individual bird.

- **Sex**: If you are able to see a sexually dimorphic species, record either "M" (male) or "F" (female) on the form; otherwise, leave blank. Leave the "sex" field blank for all auditory detections and for flocks that contain both males and females.

- **Age** (Class): If you are able to determine that a bird is a juvenile based on its plumage or vocalization, enter a "J" for Juvenile; otherwise, leave blank.

- **Prev**(ious) **Point**: This column is only used for point counts, to record whether a particular bird was already detected at a previous location along the transect. Leave it blank for line transect surveys since you will not record the same bird more than once if you see it multiple times along the transect.

- **Comments**: Record any comments that seem appropriate and that might help someone interpret and analyze the data correctly.

After the Transect Survey has been Completed

15. Enter the ending time of the transect on the bottom of the form after writing "Transect Ending Time". Review the data form and fill in all fields on the data form before departing for the next transect or sampling point. Also, search the area to ensure that no equipment is left behind.

16. Record observations of other notable plant and animal species on the separate "Incidental Observations" data form (Figure SOP 5-2).

Standard Operating Procedure (SOP) # 7

Database Design and Operation:
Data Entry, Validation, and Verification
Version 1.00 (2011)

The Microsoft Access database for the Channel Island National Park landbird monitoring protocol is compliant with the Natural Resource Database Template standards (Version 3) adopted by the national I&M program. We modified a database developed by Kristen Beaupre for the Sonoran Desert I&M Network, which included data structures and features developed by John Boetsch of the North Coast and Cascades I&M Network. The back-end data structure and many of the features of the database are common to several I&M networks within the National Park Service, which will facilitate future sharing and comparing of data and data analysis routines. Mark Langraf and Simon Kingston developed the CHIS database described here.

The database includes three files: the *LB.mdb* front-end file, *LB_BE.mdb* back-end file, and *LB_Master_Bird_List.be.mdb* file that are linked using the Backend Linking Utility in the database. The front-end file, *LB.mdb*, acts as the user interface into the back-end database and contains the forms, queries, reports, and VBA code for the application. *LB_ be.mdb*, the back-end file, contains the data tables. This configuration facilitates improvements and revisions to the database front-end application without altering the actual data structure or any of the records in the back-end data tables.

The primary table for storing bird detection data (*tbl_Detections*) contains observation information such as species, distance from observer, time of detection, age, sex, and flock size. Supporting tables include data for the location (e.g., location ID, coordinates, habitat type, elevation) and event (date, time, observers, version of the protocol that was being followed, weather conditions during the count). Species, observer names and other contact information, and attribute look-up tables provide standardized values for many data fields.

Definitions of Terms

Location – the geospatial location where the landbird data are collected, such as the x, y, and z (elevation) coordinates of a point count station, or the x, y, z coordinates for the start of a line transect.

Site – At Channel Island NP, a site is one of the islands, such as East Anacapa, San Miguel, or Santa Barbara Island. There may be multiple sampling locations (point count stations and line transects) within a site.

Tour, or Event Group – Landbird sampling at CHIS is done during a *Tour* to an island, which can last one to several days. A *Tour* (which in the database tables is called an Event Group) has a start date and an end date, which may be several days apart. Numerous point counts and/or line transects are usually sampled on a *Tour* of one island, and the *Tour* is designated by a code such as A, B, or C. If an observer moves to a different island to monitor landbirds, a new, separate *Tour* would be designated for the second island.

Event – An event is defined as a 10-minute point count or the time taken to sample a line transect, and occurs on only one day. Multiple sampling events may occur on a single day, and multiple sampling events are included within a *Tour* or Event Group.

Contact -- Person who was involved with the landbird monitoring, including Observers (those who actually conducted the bird counts) and others who assisted with recording, habitat data collection, or training. The role served by each Contact is entered into the database.

Observer – Person skilled in bird detection by sight and sound who conducts the point counts or line transect counts.

Starting the CHIS Landbird Monitoring Database

Copy the latest version of the files *LB.mdb*, *LB_BE.mdb* , and *LB_Master_Bird_List.be.mdb* to the folder that you will use as the working directory, and double-click on *LB.mdb* to start the application. Upon opening the database, an "Update Data Table Connections" pop-up screen will appear to indicate "Back-end database file(s) missing", as shown below. Click Yes to fix the connection now (this will link the three files together).

In the "Update Data Tables Connections" form (Figure SOP 7-1), click on the Browse button, select the *LB_BE.mdb* file in the folder you have put the three files into, and click *OK*. Once the two filenames appear on the form with the correct pathname to the folder, click on the Update Links button in the upper right corner of the form, and then Close the form.

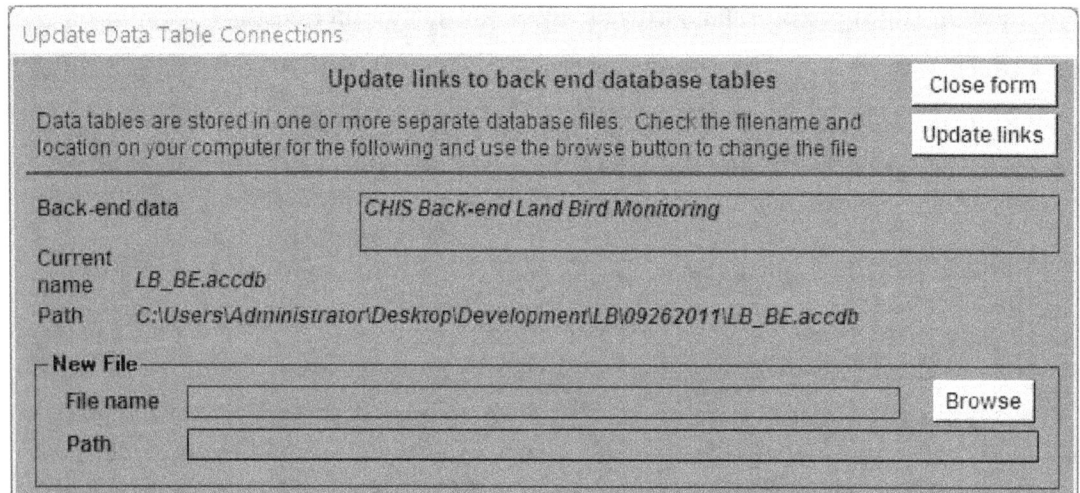

Figure SOP 7-1. Update Data Table Connections form. Using the browse buttons, find and select the LB_BE.mdb back-end data file, and then click Update Links to link the three files together.

Features of the Main Menu Form

The Main Menu form (Figure SOP 7-2) that opens when the application starts has a series of tabs across the top for the **Main** menu, **Data Maint**(enance), **Reporting** (reports and queries and data exporting), **Admin**(istration) of the database, **Defaults** values for the database, and information **About** the application. Each of the tabs will be examined in more detail in the sections that follow.

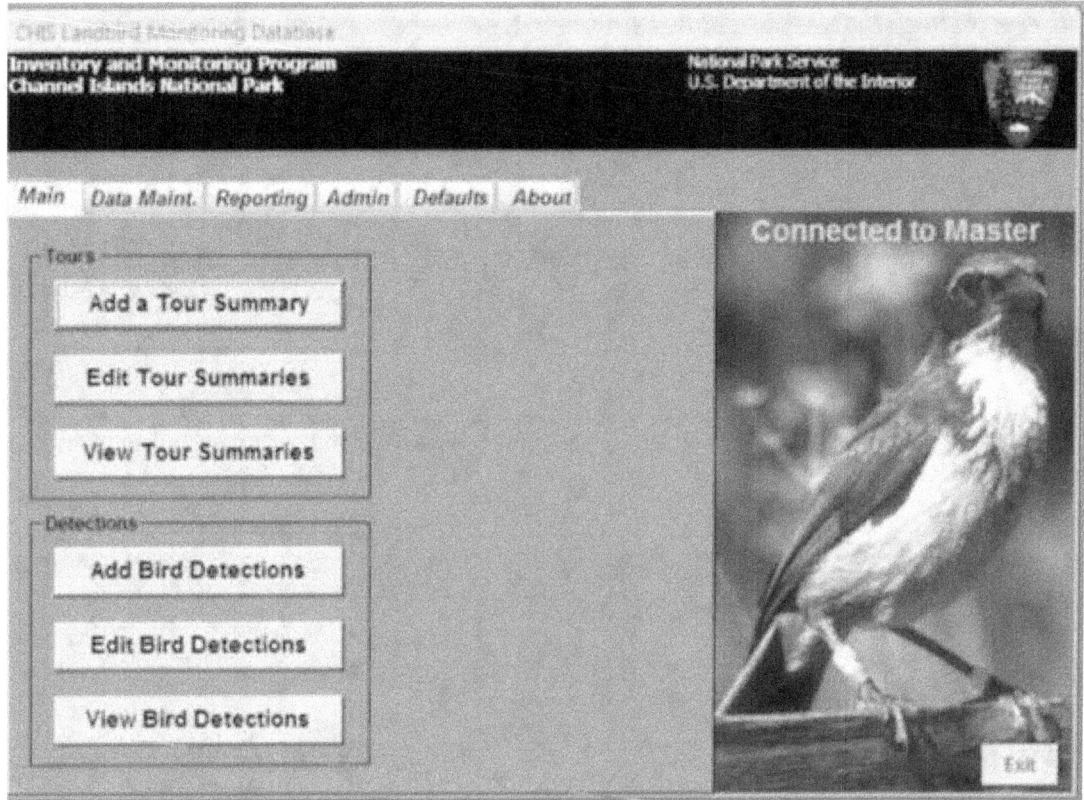

Figure SOP 7-2. Main Menu form. Separate buttons are used to View, Add, or Edit tour summary or bird detection data. Tabs across the top of the form lead to other features for Data Maintenance, Reporting, database Administration, and setting Default values.

In addition to the tabs across the top of the form, the main menu has buttons to View, Add, or Edit summary data about a tour (these were called Trip Reports in the legacy CHIS landbird database), and buttons to View, Add, or Edit bird detection data (i.e., the data collected at a point count or line transect location, such as the species, flock size, and distance from the observer). Viewing versus Editing of the data are kept separate as a Quality Assurance feature of the database to prevent someone from unintentionally changing or deleting data.

Figure SOP 7-3 below shows an example of the "View Tour Summaries" form with partial data entered for a Tour to East Anacapa Island that began on 3/8/2011 and ended on 3/9/2011, with an Event Code (also known as Tour Code) of "C". The notes field includes some overall weather data for the Tour. The database has fields available to give the Tour a name (e.g., "Spring 2011 Landbird Tour to East Anacapa Island"), a description (memo field), any notes about the Tour such as overall weather conditions, and the name or url of any filenames associated with the

Tour (e.g., this could be the filename for a "Trip Report" Word document created under the old version of the protocol). The "View Detections" form is shown in Figure SOP 7-4.

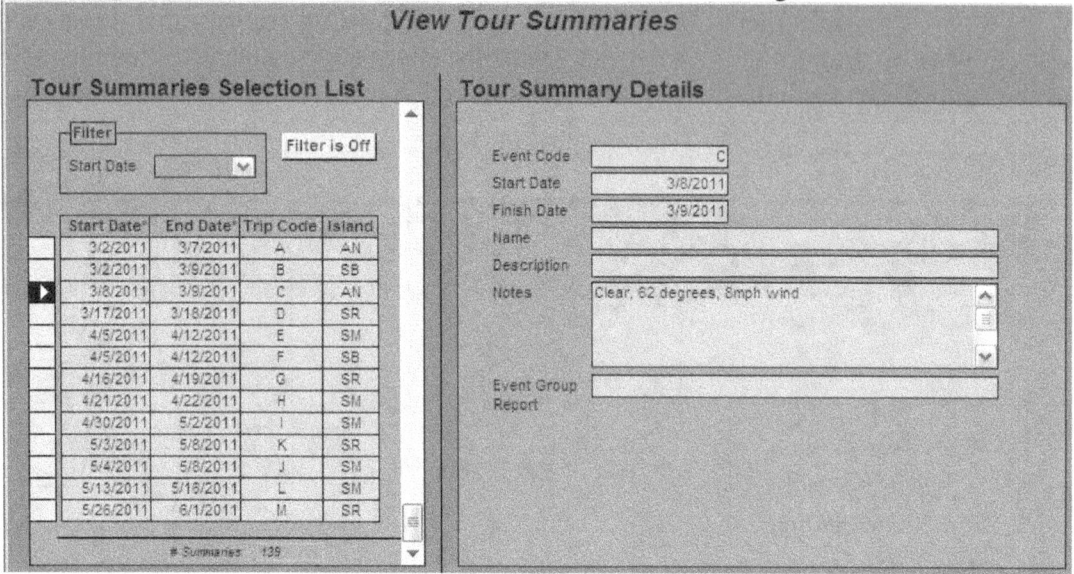

Figure SOP 7-3. Example of a "View Tour Summaries" form for a Tour to East Anacapa Island on March 8-9, 2011.

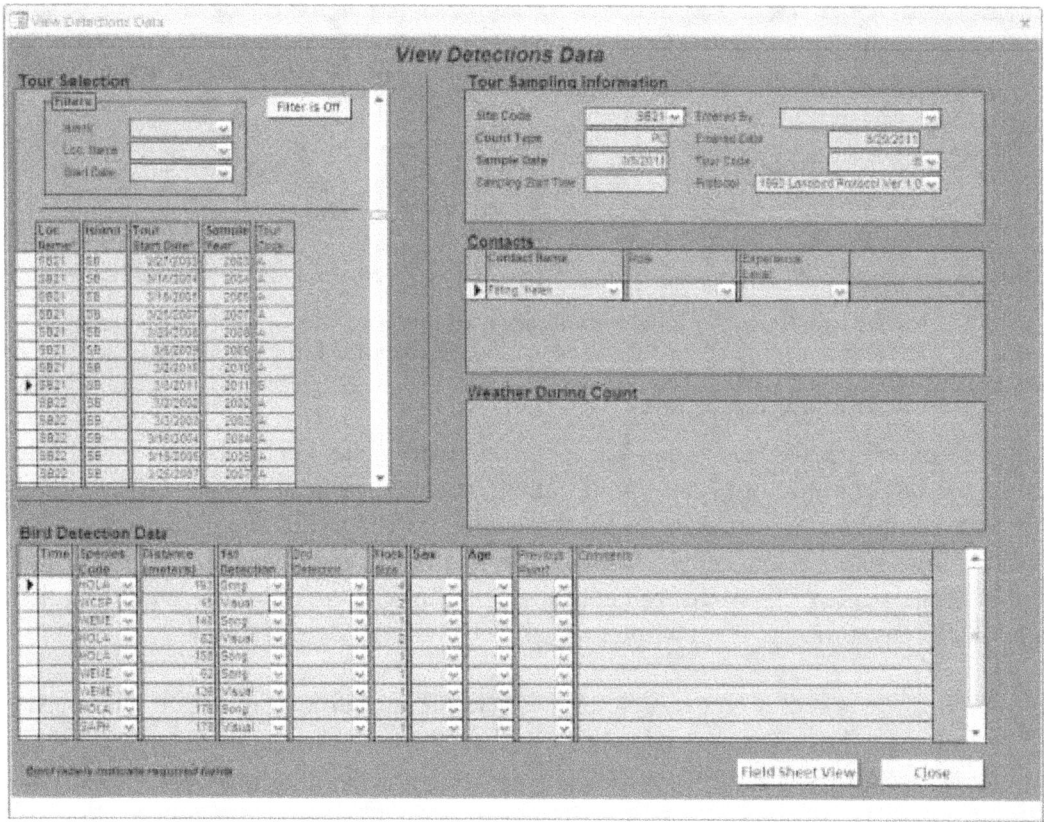

Figure 5. Example of the "View Detections" form for a 10-minute point count at Site SB21 on Santa Barbara Island on March 8, 2011. Nine flocks of birds were detected during the 10-minute count. Note the "Field Sheet View" button at the bottom right that will present a view of the data that closely matches the field data sheet.

The Bird Detection Data Entry form (Figure SOP 7-5) is used to enter data from field data sheets into the database. Although the primary goal of data entry is to transcribe all data from paper records into the database with 100% accuracy, this target is rarely achieved. To facilitate data-entry accuracy, we have built into the database many quality assurance/quality control (QA/QC) mechanisms to eliminate as many potential data-entry errors as possible. The Bird Detection Data Entry form closely matches the field data form, with location, event, and weather condition data entered at the top of the form, and data for each bird or flock of birds detected entered at the bottom of the form. Where appropriate, pick lists and range controls (upper and lower values that are acceptable) are built into the data entry form to ensure that only valid names or measures are entered. The "Field Sheet View" button will produce a view of the form that looks very similar to the field data form to assist with double-checking entries to make sure they are the same as on the paper data form.

Figure SOP 7-6. Bird Detection Data Entry form. The form is organized similar to the field data sheet, with location, event, and weather data at the top of the form, and rows at the bottom to enter data for each bird detection record.

Features of the Data Maintenance Form

The Data Maintenance tab includes features (Figure SOP 7-6) to View/Add/Edit data about point count or transect Locations, View/Add/Edit data about species in the master species list for CHIS, Add or Edit data for Observers and other Contacts (e.g., observer initials, phone number, email), and a button for Importing data from a satellite (working copy) of the database. The satellite database might be used by staff while staying overnight on one of the islands, and facilitates the importing of the data into the master database once staff return to park headquarters in Ventura.

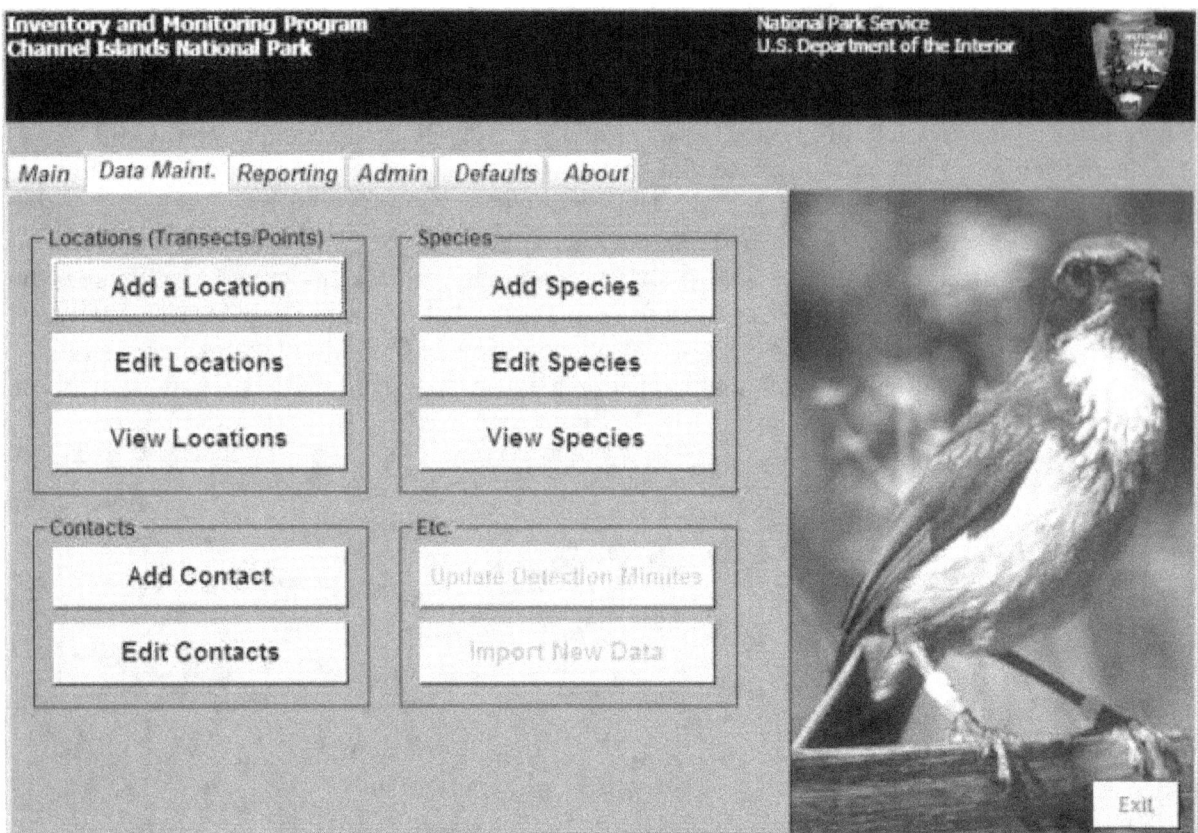

Figure SOP 7-7. The Data Maintenance form has features to View/Add/Edit data for point count or transect locations, View/Add/Edit species data for the master species list, Add/Edit observer or other contact information, and to Import data from the satellite (working copy) of the database into the master version of the database.

Features of the Reporting Form

The Reporting tab leads to some powerful reports, queries, and data export routines that will help to summarize and analyze data, and will facilitate the process for publishing annual reports and occasional trend reports. Several of the reports produce summarized data that can be cut-and-pasted into an annual report. Data export routines are built into the application to simplify the process for exporting the data into the DISTANCE software package for developing detection functions. Detailed instructions for exporting to DISTANCE are included in SOP #9 of the protocol. There is also an export routine built into the application to facilitate data export to the R statistical package to summarize data and to produce publication-quality graphics. The list below describes the purpose for each of the reports, queries, and export routines presented on the Reporting form (Figure SOP 7-7). The results of each of the reports can either be viewed on the screen ("View Report" button) or exported to an Excel file ("Report to Excel" button).

<u>Available Reports and Queries:</u>
- **Detailed List of Sampling Locations and Dates** – This report provides a list of all point counts or line transects sampled on all islands, sorted by Island, Year, Tour Code, and then Location ID. The location type (Point Count or Line Transect) and the predominant habitat type for the Point Count or Line Transect are also listed for each location listed.

- **List of Observers and Other Contacts** – This report, sorted by Observer initials, lists the last name, first name, middle initial, and email address for all contacts entered into the database.

- **Number of Transects and Points by Island and Date** – This report lists the Island, Tour Code, Start Date, End Date, number of line transects sampled during the tour, and number of point counts sampled during the tour, for all sampling tours on all islands since 1993.

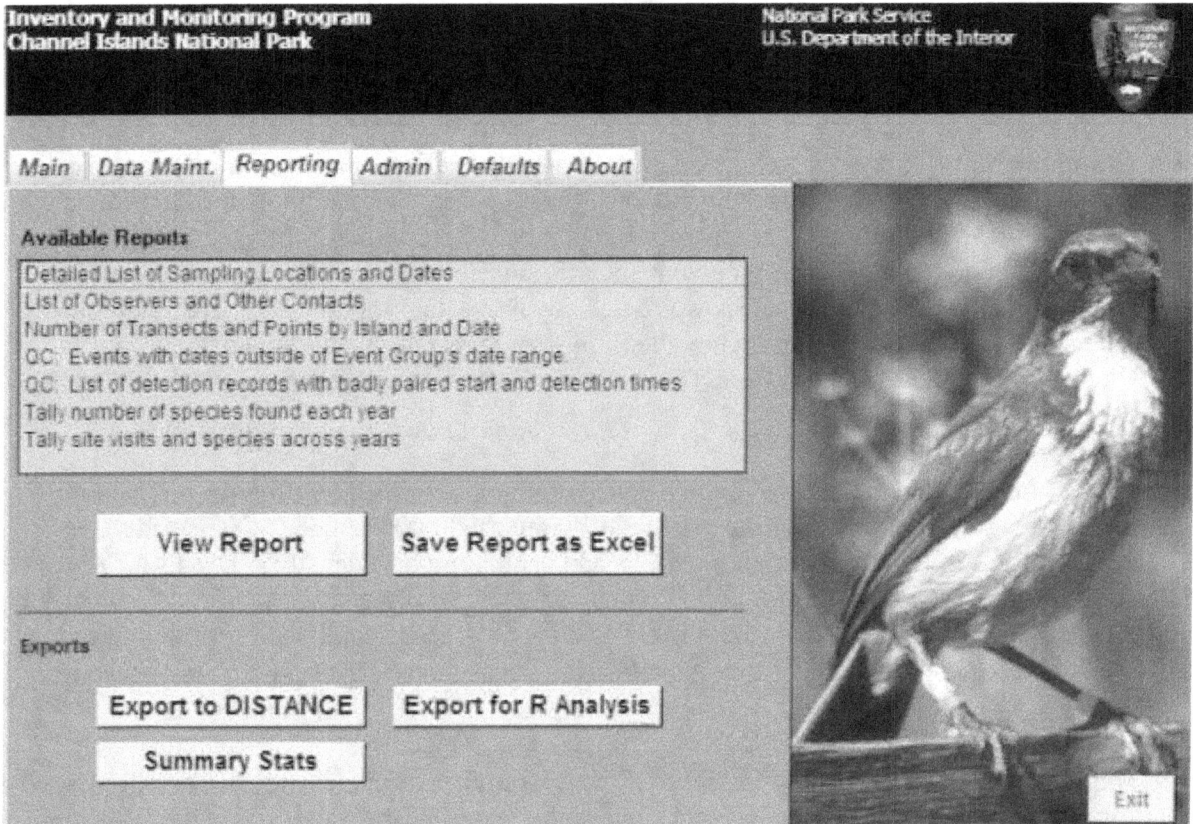

Figure SOP 7-8. Form for running reports, queries, and data export routines. A short description of each report, query, and export routine is presented in this SOP.

- **QC: Events with dates outside of Event Group's data range** – This is a data quality-checking query that will list any sampling dates that occur before the start date or after the end data of a Tour on a particular island.

- **QC: List of detection records with badly paired start and detection times** – This data quality-checking query lists records that do not have a valid detection time, and records for which the detection time is not within 10 minutes of the start time of a point count, and line transect records that do not fall between the start and end time of the line transect.

- **Tally number of species found each year** – For each year beginning in 1993, this report lists the total number of individuals of each species that were detected during point counts or line transects. The report lists the four-character AOU code for each bird species detected that year, common name, scientific name, order, family, and total number of individuals detected.

- **Tally site visits and species across years** – For each year beginning in 1993, this report lists the number of islands on which landbird monitoring was conducted, the number of unique point count stations or line transects sampled, the total number of locations sampled (i.e., some point counts or line transects may have been sampled more than once during the year, especially in the early 90s when spring and fall counts were conducted), and the total number of bird species detected during point counts or line transects.

Data Export Routines:

- **Summary Stats** – For point counts conducted during a selected landbird monitoring Tour, this data summary routine calculates for each bird species, the total number of individuals detected, the mean and standard error for the number of individuals of that species detected per point count, the number of plots on which the species was detected, and the percent of plots sampled on which the species was detected. These data should greatly facilitate the production of an annual report. When the Summary Stats button is selected, a pop-up window will request the Island and Tour Start Date for which the summary statistics are to be calculated.

- **Export to Distance** – The Export to Distance routine produces a text file for point count or line transect data that is formatted to be readily imported into the DISTANCE software package for developing detection functions and estimating bird densities. DISTANCE has separate analysis procedures for point counts versus line transects, so the routine produces a different type of output file for these two count types. A more detailed description of the procedure for importing data from the landbird database into DISTANCE is presented in SOP #9.

- **Export for R Analysis** – This export routine will produce an Excel file with data formatted for analysis using the R statistical package or other external software. The excel file should be saved as a .csv (comma-separated values) text file. SOP #8, Data Summary, Analysis, and Reporting, contains R scripts that will read this .csv file and can be used to summarize data and produce publication-quality graphics for annual reports and the occasional trend report.

Features of the Application Administration Form

The **Admin** tab on the Main Menu leads to the form shown in Figure SOP 7-8 below, in which the user can manage data in lookup tables, enter or edit data for different versions of the protocol, produce a backup file with all of the data, connect the data tables if this has not already been done when the application starts, and create a blank "satellite" working copy of the database for the purpose of remote data entry.

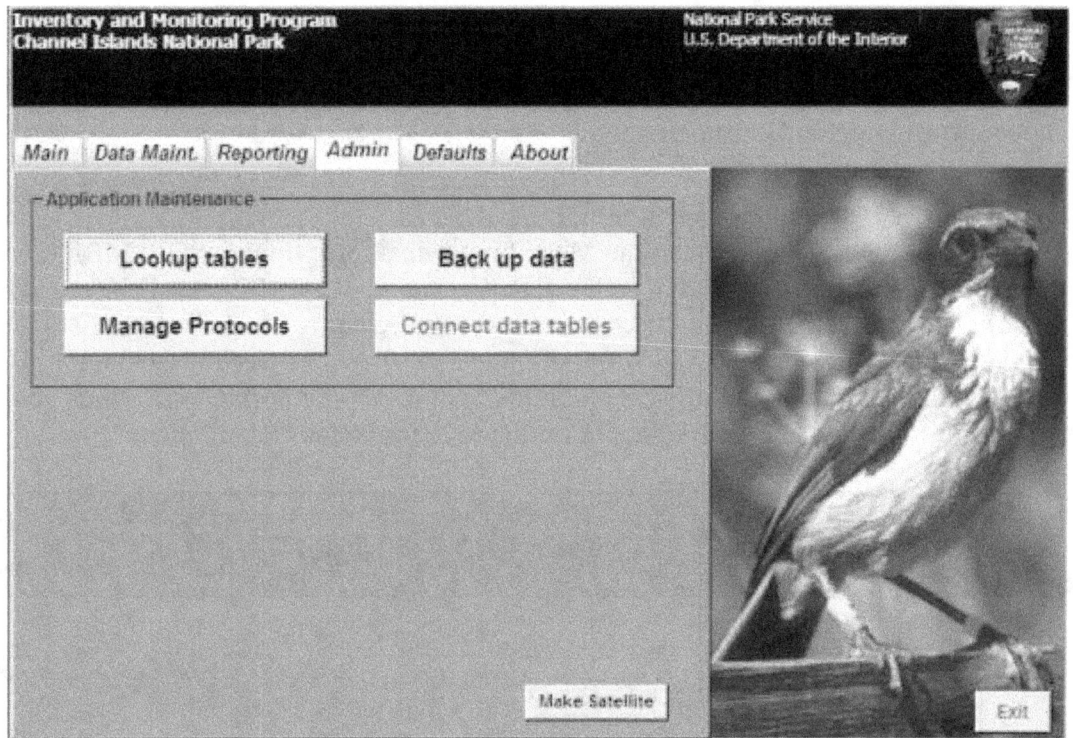

Figure SOP 7-9. Application Administration Form is used to maintain lookup tables, create a backup data file, and create a blank "satellite" database for remote data entry.

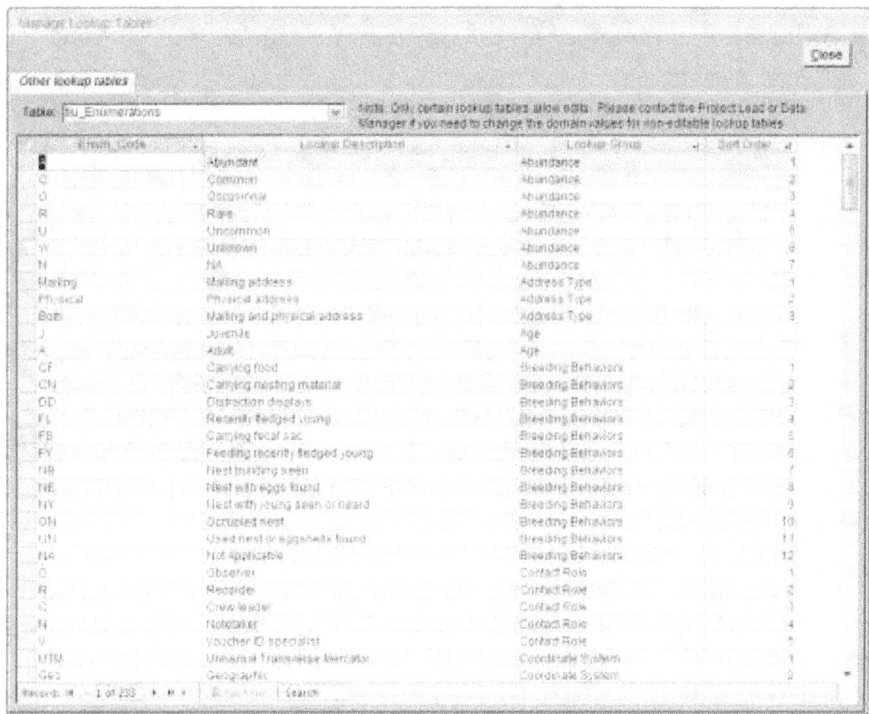

Figure SOP 7-10. The table tlu_Enumerations contains most of the lookup data for pick lists and data field names.

Most of the data contained in lookup tables and picklists is contained in the table tlu_Enumerations as shown in Figure SOP 7-9. Some of the entries have been locked and can only be edited or deleted by the Project Manager or network Data Manager to guard against unintentional corrupting of the data set.

Features of the Defaults Form

Clicking on the Defaults tab from the Main Menu brings up a form (Figure SOP 7-10) where the database Default values are set. To change User, Park, Datum, or UTM Zone, click the *Change* button to bring up the Defaults form. Each value can be selected from a drop-down list. If you are unable to find a User, click the *New user* button to add a new one (see the Contact information in the definition of terms section of this SOP for more information). When you have finished entering default values, click the *OK* button to return to the Default menu.

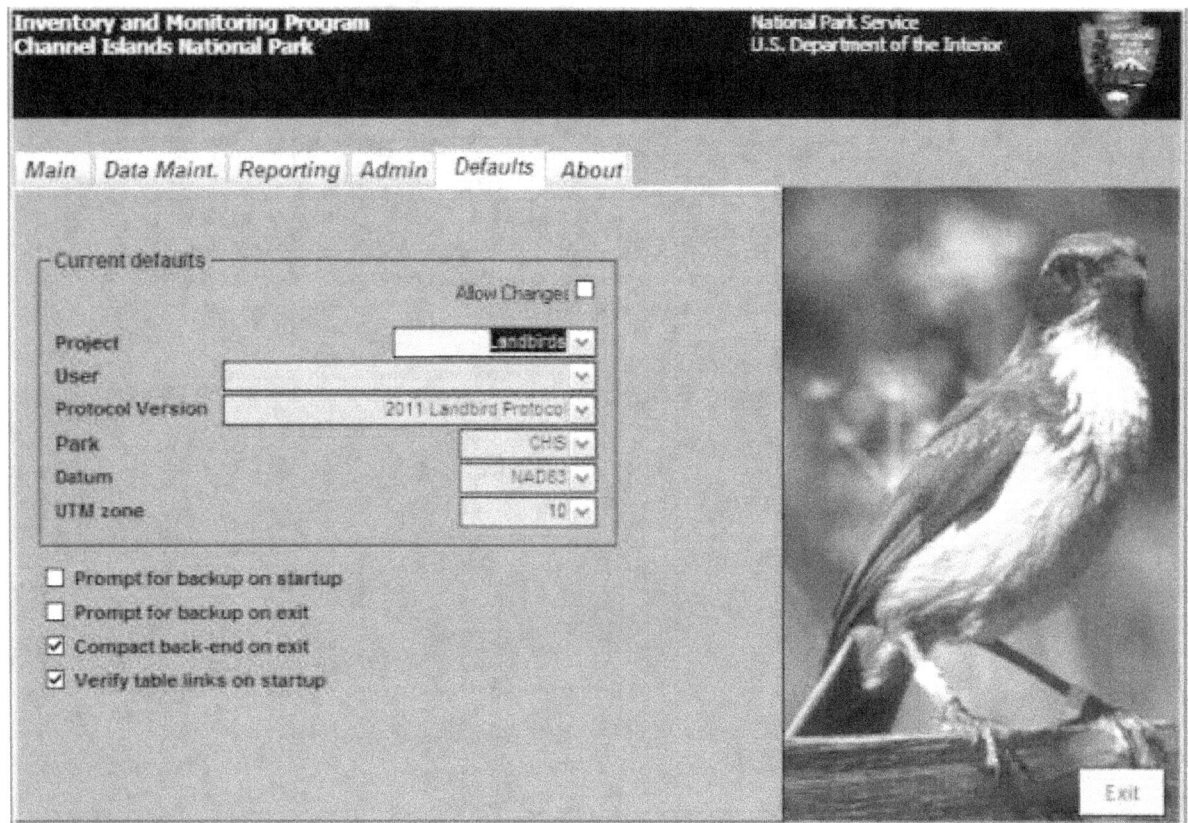

Figure SOP 7-11. Default values are viewed or edited under the Defaults tab. The "Allow Changes" box must be checked for values to be edited.

The application can be set to automatically prompt for backups every time it is started and/or every time it is closed using the *Exit* button on the main form. Making backups before and after data entry sessions is a good habit to get into, in case of database corruption or data entry mistakes.

Compaction is a process whereby Microsoft Access optimizes the organization of the file, making it smaller and quicker to access data. If you check the option to Compact back-end on exit (recommended), the application will compact the data file that is linked to the front-end when the application is closed using the Exit button on the main form.

Verify Table Links on Startup - The application is structured with a front-end (user interface) and a back-end (data tables). In order for the application to work properly, the front-end must be linked to the tables in the back-end. If this check box is checked (recommended), the link to the back-end file(s) will be checked when the application is started.

Data Entry, Verification and Validation Procedures

The Project Manager is responsible for making sure all datasheets are complete and accurate and that data is entered properly into the database. The database has a user-friendly interface to facilitate data entry and checking (verification). Data verification is the process of ensuring the data entered into a database correspond with the data recorded on the hardcopy field forms. Once the data have been entered and saved, the Project Manager and MEDN Data Manager will validate the data by reviewing the data for quality, completeness, and logical consistency. Data validation requires a reviewer to have extensive knowledge of what the data mean and how they were collected. Queries and reports have been built to look for apparent outliers, inconsistencies in entry, null values, or any other anomalous data points. Anomalies are reported to the Project Manager for resolution. Unresolved anomalies will be documented and included in the metadata and certification report. Any questions about the data, data entry procedures, or difficulties with the database are to be resolved by the Project Manager and MEDN Data Manager.

Once all verification and validation methods have been implemented, the working database will be transferred to the MEDN Data Manager, who will upload them to the master database. While uploading the data to the database, the data will be subjected to an automated data quality process that will flag potential missing sites and invalid or improperly formatted data.

Data Certification and Delivery

Data certification is a benchmark in the project information management process that indicates that 1) the data are complete for the period of record; 2) they have undergone and passed the quality assurance checks; and 3) that they are appropriately documented and in a condition for archiving, posting, and distribution. Certification is not intended to imply that the data are completely free of errors or inconsistencies which may not have been detected during quality assurance reviews. Rather, it describes a formal and standardized process to track and minimize errors.

To ensure that only data of the highest possible quality are included in reports and other project deliverables, the data certification step is an annual requirement for all tabular and spatial data. The Project Manager is primarily responsible for completing certification. The completed form, certified data, and updated metadata should be delivered to the MEDN Data Manager according to the specified timeline.

Metadata Procedures

Data documentation is a critical step toward ensuring that datasets are useable for their intended purposes well into the future. This involves the development of metadata, which can be defined as structured information about the content, quality, and condition of data. Additionally, metadata provide the means to catalog datasets within intranet and internet systems, making data more accessible to a broad range of potential users. Metadata for all MEDN monitoring data will conform to Federal Geographic Data Committee (FGDC) and NPS guidelines and will contain all components of supporting information such that the data may be confidently manipulated, analyzed, and synthesized. For long-term projects such as this one, metadata creation is most time consuming the first time it is developed – after which most information remains static from one year to the next. Metadata records in subsequent years then only need to be updated to reflect current publications, references, taxonomic conventions, contact information, data disposition and quality, and to describe any changes in collection methods, analysis approaches or quality assurance for the project.

Specific procedures for metadata development and posting are outlined in the MEDN Data Management Plan. In general, the Project Lead and MEDN Data Manager will work together to create and update an FGDC- and NPS-compliant metadata record in XML format. The Project Manager should update the metadata content as changes to the protocol are made, and each year as additional data are accumulated. Edits within the document should be tracked so that any changes are obvious to those who will use it to update the XML metadata file. The MEDN Data Manager will facilitate metadata development by creating and parsing metadata records, and by posting such records to the NPS IRMA (Integrated Resource Management Applications) data system where they will be available to the public.

Channel Islands National Park Landbird Monitoring Protocol

Standard Operating Procedure (SOP) # 8

Data Summary, Analysis, and Reporting
Version 1.00 (2011)

This Standard Operating Procedure (SOP) provides specific procedures and tips for presenting a simple summary of each year's monitoring results in an annual report, and for analyzing the landbird data and producing summary tables and a series of graphics for occasional trend and synthesis reports. To streamline and simplify the reporting process, the majority of the routine data summary and graphing procedures have either been built into the *LB.mdb* database, or else are performed with the R statistical package using a series of R scripts that are contained in companion files including CHIS_R_Scripts_BPS.R and CHIS_R_Scripts_DISTANCE.R. The BPS file contains scripts that generate tables and graphics for summarizing abundance (e.g., birds per station), occurrence (e.g., percent of stations where a particular species was detected), and species richness. The DISTANCE.R scripts produce histograms and boxplots to help evaluate the effect of different covariates on detection distances, and to summarize detection distances for each species, prior to modeling the data in the software package DISTANCE. It is not necessary for the user to know how to program in R in order to use the R scripts.

At least once each year, usually between November and February after the field season has concluded and data have been entered into the *LB.mdb* database and certified, the Project Manager should publish an annual report in the NPS Natural Resource Data Series (NRDS) to summarize the year's monitoring results. The description for the Natural Resource Data Series (http://www.nature.nps.gov/publications/nrpm) says that it is "intended for the timely release of basic data sets and data summaries. An example would be simple, annual reporting of monitoring results that will be more thoroughly analyzed and interpreted later as part of a multi-year trend report. Care is taken to assure accuracy of raw data values, but a thorough analysis and interpretation of the data has not been completed. Consequently, the initial analyses of data in these reports are provisional and subject to change". An example of an annual report for landbird monitoring that follows this protocol has been published as Coonan et al. (2011) to demonstrate how the data summaries produced by the database and by the R scripts can be used to quickly (e.g., less than one day for most annual reports) produce an annual report in the NRDS series. The 2011 annual report example was produced in less than two hours using the following components:

1. Table 1 in the annual report summarizes the number of line transects and point counts conducted on each island during 2011, and provides the sampling dates. The data were produced by the database report "Number of Transects and Points by Island and Date". The report was exported to excel, and the 2011 sampling events were extracted and entered into a table in Word using the template and styles for the Natural Resource Data Series.

2. Table 2 summarizes the number of individuals of each species detected during bird surveys on all islands in 2011, with the common name, scientific names, and species code for each species. This was produced by taking the 2011 records from the database report "Tally of Species Found each Year".

3. Tables 3 through 6 in the annual report summarize the abundance (birds per station) and occupancy (percent of stations on which a particular species was detected) for each species on each island, and was produced by Section 1 of the R scripts. First, a .csv (comma-separated values) text file was created by exporting all data in the database using the "Export for R Analysis" report function in the database, and then renaming the file as "CHISbird.csv". Section 1 of the R scripts reads the "CHISbird.csv" file, removes unknown species and seabirds (since they are monitored by a separate protocol and have not been recorded consistently during landbird counts over the years), calculates the summary statistics, opens a blank Word document, and then produces a series of data summary tables in Word for all combinations of season, island, and year. The tables for 2011 were then cut and pasted into the 2011 annual report and formatting styles applied.

4. Figures 1 and 2 in the annual report are boxplots produced by Section 1 of the R scripts to show the 2011 mean abundance for each species in context to all data since 1993 (for point counts only).

5. Figures 3 through 5 were also produced by Section 1 of the R scripts to show patterns of species occupancy on each island since 1993. These graphs can be used to answer the questions, "are any new species starting to show up on an island, or are we no longer detection certain species that used to be here"?

6. Finally, a few sentences were written to describe some of the sampling events and results for 2011 and voila!, an annual report was produced in less than two hours.

At least once every five years, or more often as needed to address a particular management issue or question, a multi-year trend and synthesis report should be developed that summarizes and interprets all of the landbird data collected at CHIS since 1993. These multi-year reports should be published in the NPS Natural Resource Technical Report or Natural Resource Report series. The data summary and export routines that are built into the database, and the R scripts that accompany this protocol, will streamline the development of these multi-year trend reports. The multi-year reports should include an analysis of the use of different habitat types by landbirds, and trends in occupancy and abundance by habitat type. The multi-year reports should also include a detailed analysis of bird densities based on the development of detection functions for each species using the program DISTANCE, after investigating the effect of covariates such as Observer, Habitat, Season, and weather variables on bird detection data. The DISTANCE.R scripts will help to streamline the process for inspecting detection distances and evaluating the effect of covariates on detection distances to help determine how best to model data for each species in the DISTANCE software. Different approaches are needed for the initial analysis of line transect data versus point count data because of differences in the amount of area that is being sampled by each method, but the results from the two methods can be combined and compared in the multi-year trend reports. The R package UNMARKED, can be used to analyze and model line transect data collected using this protocol without having to import the data into DISTANCE to do the analysis and modeling. An R package has not yet been developed that will allow point count data to be analyzed entirely in R, and so the methods outlined in SOP #9 in this protocol should be used to import the data into DISTANCE for modeling of detection functions.

All reports should be uploaded to the IRMA (Integrated Resource Management Applications) data system, and links to them should be posted on the MEDN network website.

R Scripts

The following R scripts read the CHISbird.csv file that is exported by the LB.mdb database, and produces a series of data summary tables and graphics that can be used in annual reports and multi-year trend and synthesis reports:

```
 R scripts for summarizing landbird monitoring data for Channel Islands National Park
# Most recently updated December 14, 2011
##########################################################################
#                                                                        #
# Section 1. Summarize birds detected per station sampled, and percent of stations at   #
#         which a particular species was detected during point counts. Open a Word      #
#         file and output summary tables. Open a .pdf document and output a series      #
#         of graphics summarizing species abundance data by island.                    #
#                                                                        #
##########################################################################


# set the working directory to the folder with the data file (you will need to edit this)
setwd("c:/CHIS_Landbirds")

library(ggplot2)
library(xtable)  # output formatting for Table 1
library(R2wd)    # library for exporting tables to Word
rm(list=ls())    # clear and reset the R workspace to remove stored data from previous runs

# Read the .csv file to get the names of the variables from the header, and the data
RawData <- read.csv("CHISbird.csv",header=TRUE,as.is=TRUE) # read file, don't convert strings to factors

# convert StartDate and EndDate to Dates
RawData$StartDate <- as.Date(RawData$StartDate,format="%m/%d/%Y")
RawData$EndDate <- as.Date(RawData$EndDate,format="%m/%d/%Y")
names(RawData)[13] <- "Year" #change the name of the variable Yr to Year for later use

# Make lookup table of 4-character species codes and Common Name of each species
SPlist <- unique(RawData[,c("Species","Common_Name")])


##########################################################################
#
# Calculate Summary Statistics for each Island-Year-Season Combination for Point Counts only
# This code determines whether a particular Site was sampled in a particular Year and Season.
# We first create a single Index variable compounded from only the existing combinations
# of Survey, Site, Season, and Start_Date, then table(Index,Species) to make a skeleton of
# all species by Index combinations, set those counts to zero, glue that skeleton of zeros
# to the observed, data, sum by Index and Species (summing the 0 with the observed count),
# then parse back out the Island, Survey, and Season. Start_Date is added to the index because
# some stations may be sampled on more than one tour within a season in cases where multiple
# tours are made to an island within a season.

# PointCounts is a subset of the raw data in the .csv input file using only point count data
```

```
PointCounts <- RawData[RawData$Loc_Type=="PC",]

# Make Index variable of all Survey & Site & Season combinations for which at least 1 bird was detected
PointCounts$Index <-
paste(PointCounts$Survey,PointCounts$Site,PointCounts$Season,PointCounts$Start_Date,sep="_")

# Remove unknown species and seabird species from the data set. Seabirds are sampled by
# another protocol. The ! means NOT, so the species in DropList will be removed from RawData
DropList <-
c("UNKN","NONE","UNSC","GULL","CORM","BRCO","DCCO","PECO","HUMM","WEGU","BRPE")
PointCounts <- PointCounts[!PointCounts$Species%in%DropList,]

# For the calculations of birds per station, also remove birds that were "flyovers" and were
# not associated with the particular plot. This includes any bird with distance less than zero
PointCounts <- PointCounts[!PointCounts$Distance<0,]

# make skeleton table of Index by Species and fill it with zeros to initiate
Skeleton <- data.frame(with(PointCounts,table(Index,Species)))
names(Skeleton)[3] <- "Cluster_Size" #third variable in the Skeleton table is now the cluster size
Skeleton$Cluster_Size <- 0

#append Skeleton of zeros to PointCounts, then aggregate by Index and Species
temp <- rbind(Skeleton,PointCounts[,c(27,20,25)])
data1 <- aggregate(Cluster_Size~Index+Species,data=temp,FUN=sum)
rm(temp)
names(data1) <- c("Index","Species","Cluster_Size")
data1$Index <- as.character(data1$Index)
data1$Island <- substr(data1$Index,1,2)
data1$Survey <- substr(data1$Index,1,7)

# To find Season in the Index variable, extract out the first four characters that follow the second
# underscore character, which will return either Spri or Fall
flag <- regexpr("_",substr(data1$Index,9,nchar(data1$Index))) +9 # position after second underscore
data1$Season <- substr(data1$Index,flag,flag+3)
data1$Season[which(data1$Season=="Spri")] <- "Spring"

# number of birds detected
SumSpp <- aggregate(Cluster_Size~Species+Season+Survey,data=data1,FUN=sum)

# mean density
MeanSpp <- aggregate(Cluster_Size~Species+Season+Survey,data=data1,FUN=mean)

# sd mean density
SdSpp <- aggregate(Cluster_Size~Species+Season+Survey,data=data1,FUN=sd)

# using table() to count records would fill in extra zeros, so summing
# the logical Cluster_Size>0 (1 for true) in aggregate is easier

# stations present
```

```
StationPresences <- aggregate(Cluster_Size>0~Species+Season+Survey,data=data1,FUN=sum)
names(StationPresences)[4] <-"N.Present"
data1$One <- 1
NStations <- aggregate(One~Species+Season+Survey,data=data1,FUN=sum)

# Because all 4 dataframes came from aggregate with the same right-side formula
# on the same data, they all have the same number of observations in the same order,
# so we can glue on columns with data.frame() instead of merging by pairs of dataframes
Table1 <- data.frame(SumSpp,MeanSpp$Cluster_Size,SdSpp$Cluster_Size,
                     StationPresences$N.Present,NStations$One)

names(Table1) <- c("Species","Season","Survey","N.Detected","Mean","SD",
                   "StationsPresent","NStations")
Table1$SE <- Table1$SD / sqrt(Table1$NStations)
Table1$Pct <- Table1$StationsPresent / Table1$NStations * 100
Table1$Year <- substr(Table1$Survey,4,7)
Table1$Island <- substr(Table1$Survey,1,2)

# Table1 now contains the following summary statistics for Point Counts for each species for
# each Island-Year-Season combination: Species, Survey, Total number detected, Mean birds
# per station, Standard Deviation, Number of stations where the bird was present,
# Number of stations counted on that tour, Standard Error of the Mean, and Percent of
# stations on which the species was detected.

# For Spring season and for each species, count the total number of birds detected on all
# islands combined and all years combined. This will be used to sort species by abundance.
SumDetections <- aggregate(N.Detected~Species,data=Table1[Table1$Season=="Spring",],FUN=sum)
Table1 <- merge(Table1,SumDetections, by="Species")
names(Table1)[4] <-"SurveyN"
names(Table1)[13] <-"SumN"

# SumN now contains the total Spring detections for each species across all islands and years

Table1 <- merge(Table1,SPlist,by.x="Species",by.y="Species",all.x=TRUE)

# Now export Table 1 to a .csv file called BirdsPerStation.csv
write.csv(Table1, file = "BirdsPerStation.csv")

##############################################################################
#
# Code for exporting summarized Birds per Station and Occurrence data to tables in Word
# Use R2wd package to create an MS Word document with summary tables by Island, Season, Year
#
# make data.frame of tour start & stop dates and numbers of plots for each tour using unique
Tours <- unique(RawData[,c(1,7,10:13)])
Tours <- Tours[order(Tours$Island,Tours$Year,Tours$Season,Tours$StartDate),c(1,2,5,6,3,4)]

# Create table headers for each new Island and Season
# \t is tab character; this is set up for appearance as text
```

```
TableHeader <- paste("\tTotal\t\tBirds per Station\t# Stations\tPercent\n",
  "Species\tDetected\tMean\tSE\t\tPresent\t\tOccupied\n\n",sep="")
SSlist <- unique(Table1[,c(2:3,8)]) # unique combinations of Season, Island, and Year
SSlist <- SSlist[with(SSlist, order(Season, Survey)), ]

# Open an MS Word document
wdGet()

# Loop through each Season-Survey combination (Spring and Fall) and export table to Word
for (ss in 1:nrow(SSlist)) {
  tSurvey <- SSlist$Survey[ss]
  tSeason <- SSlist$Season[ss]
  OutTable <- subset(Table1,Survey==tSurvey&Season==tSeason&SurveyN>0)
  OutTable <- OutTable[,c(1,14,4,5,9,7,10)]
  names(OutTable) <-  c("Species","Common Name","#Detected","Mean per Stn","S.E.","# Stns","% Stns")
  OutTable[,4] <- round(OutTable[,4],digits=2)  # trim digits
  OutTable[,5] <- round(OutTable[,5],digits=2)
  OutTable[,7] <- round(OutTable[,7],digits=1)
  OutX <- xtable(OutTable, include.rownames = FALSE, floating = FALSE) # create xtable object

# header information
metaTable2 <- matrix(nrow=2,ncol=2,data=c(
        paste("Island:",substr(tSurvey,1,2)),
        paste("Number of Plots:",SSlist$NStations[ss]),
        paste("Season:",tSeason),
        paste("Year:",substr(tSurvey,4,7))),
        byrow=TRUE )
mt2 <- paste("Island:",substr(tSurvey,1,2),"\tNumber of Stations:",SSlist$NStations[ss],
              "\tSeason:",tSeason,"\tYear:",substr(tSurvey,4,7))
# write header, then table
# page header
wdSubsection(title="Summary Statistics by Season, Island, and Year",
    label=paste(tSurvey,tSeason,sep="_"), newpage=FALSE)
wdHeading(level=3,text=mt2)
wdTable(OutTable,autoformat=1)
 } # end of loop for ss


###################################################################################
###################################################################################
#
# Code for plotting mean Birds per Station results for each species and each year,
# with one .png graphic for each island. The dot on the graph with the triangle around it is
# the mean BPS for the most recent year, to show how it compares to means for other years
# that are summarized by the boxplot.

# Make the .png plots 8 inches high by 6 inches wide, with resolution 200 dpi
png("MeanBPS_AN.png", res=200, width=6, height=8, units="in")
d1=Table1[Table1$Island=="AN"&Table1$Season=="Spring",]
d1=d1[d1$SumN>2&d1$Mean>0,]     # Species with at least two detections in all years and mean >0
```

```
d1$Species <- as.character(d1$Species)
d1 <- merge(d1,SPlist,by.x="Species",by.y="Species",all.x=TRUE)

# Now get the mean birds per station for 2011 so that it can be compared to past years' mean BPS
d2 <- d1[d1$Year==2011, ]

p1 <- qplot(Common_Name, Mean, data=d1, ylab="Mean Birds per Station",
        xlab="Species", main="East Anacapa Island") + geom_boxplot()
p2 <- p1 + geom_point(data=d2, aes(x=Common_Name, y=Mean, cex=3,
        pch=24)) + opts(legend.position = "none")+ coord_flip()
print(p2)
dev.off()

png("MeanBPS_SB.png", res=200, width=6, height=8, units="in")
d1=Table1[Table1$Island=="SB"&Table1$Season=="Spring",]
d1=d1[d1$SumN>2&d1$Mean>0,]    # Species with at least two detections in all years and mean >0
d1$Species <- as.character(d1$Species)
d1 <- merge(d1,SPlist,by.x="Species",by.y="Species",all.x=TRUE)

# Now get the mean birds per station for 2011 so that it can be compared to past years' mean BPS
d2 <- d1[d1$Year==2011, ]

p1 <- qplot(Common_Name, Mean, data=d1, ylab="Mean Birds per Station",
        xlab="Species", main="Santa Barbara Island") + geom_boxplot()
p2 <- p1 + geom_point(data=d2, aes(x=Common_Name, y=Mean, cex=3,
        pch=24)) + opts(legend.position = "none")+ coord_flip()
print(p2)
dev.off()

# This code doesn't work for Santa Cruz Island because there was no data collected in 2011, so skip

png("MeanBPS_SM.png", res=200, width=6, height=8, units="in") # make the graph 8 inches high by 6 inches
wide
d1=Table1[Table1$Island=="SM"&Table1$Season=="Spring",]
d1=d1[d1$SumN>2&d1$Mean>0,] # Species with at least two detections in all years and mean >0
d1$Species <- as.character(d1$Species)
d1 <- merge(d1,SPlist,by.x="Species",by.y="Species",all.x=TRUE)

# Now get the mean birds per station for 2011 so that it can be compared to past years' mean BPS
d2 <- d1[d1$Year==2011, ]

p1 <- qplot(Common_Name, Mean, data=d1,
        ylab="Mean Birds per Station", xlab="Species", main="San Miguel Island") + geom_boxplot()
p2 <- p1 + geom_point(data=d2, aes(x=Common_Name, y=Mean, cex=3,
        pch=24)) + opts(legend.position = "none")+ coord_flip()
print(p2)
dev.off()
```

```
png("MeanBPS_SR.png", res=200, width=6, height=8, units="in") # make the graph 8 inches high by 6 inches
wide
d1=Table1[Table1$Island=="SR"&Table1$Season=="Spring",]
d1=d1[d1$SumN>2&d1$Mean>0,] # Species with at least two detections in all years and mean >0
d1$Species <- as.character(d1$Species)
d1 <- merge(d1,SPlist,by.x="Species",by.y="Species",all.x=TRUE)


# Now get the mean birds per station for 2011 so that it can be compared to past years' mean BPS
d2 <- d1[d1$Year==2011, ]

p1 <- qplot(Common_Name, Mean, data=d1,
        ylab="Mean Birds per Station", xlab="Species", main="Santa Rosa Island") + geom_boxplot()
p2 <- p1 + geom_point(data=d2, aes(x=Common_Name, y=Mean, cex=3,
        pch=24)) + opts(legend.position = "none")+ coord_flip()
print(p2)
dev.off()


###################################################################################
###################################################################################
#
# Code for plotting out multi-panel graphs, one for each species, showing Birds Per Station
# with Standard Error bars on one graph, and Percent of Stations occupied on a second graph.
# The series of graphs are output to a .pdf file called BPS.pdf
# This may take 10 minutes or more to run since it loops through every species detected.
#
# Calculate how many different species there are to loop through
spList=unique(Table1$Species)
Nsp=length(spList) # n is now the number of species for all islands combined (point counts only)

# Resort Table1 so that the most commonly-detected species come first in the data frame
  Table1 <- Table1[order(-Table1$SumN), ]

# Open a .pdf file
pdf("BPS.pdf") # print plots to a pdf file that will be in the working directory

# Loop through each of the species and produce a multi-panel plot of Birds Per Station by Year
# with one sub-panel for each of the five islands. If an island was sampled and zero birds of that
# species was detected, a dot is plotted to show zero birds detected. Next, produce a bar chart
# of percent of stations occupied for each species and also print it to the .pdf file
# The following code is for Spring surveys only.

for (sp in 1:Nsp){
    SPname <- SPlist$Common_Name[which(SPlist$Species==spList[sp])]
    data2 = Table1[Table1$Species==spList[sp], ] # Loop through each of the species
    data2 = data2[data2$Season=="Spring",]  # Spring counts only

    p=ggplot(aes(x=Year, y=Mean, ymin=Mean-SE, ymax=Mean+SE), data=data2) + geom_pointrange()+
        geom_point() + facet_grid(Island ~ .) + ylab("Mean Birds per Station")+
```

```
        opts(title=paste(SPname," - Birds Per Station"))
    print(p)

    p=ggplot(aes(x=Year, y=Pct), data=data2) + geom_bar() + facet_grid(Island ~ .)+
        ylab("Percent of Stations Where Species was Detected")+
        opts(title=paste(SPname," - Percent of Stations Where Detected"))
    print(p)
}      # end of the loop through each of the species
dev.off()  # close the BPS.pdf file
```

```
##########################################################################
#                                                                        #
#  Section 2. Summarize and produce graphics for Species Richness, defined as the number  #
#          of different species detected on either line transects or point counts on      #
#          a particular island on a particular year.                     #
#                                                                        #
##########################################################################
```

```
# Use the RawData input file, since it contains both Line Transects and Point Counts
# Remove unknown species and seabird species from the data set. Seabirds are sampled by
# another protocol and have not been recorded consistently by different observers over
# the years. The ! means NOT, so the species in DropList will be removed from RawData
DropList <-
c("UNKN","NONE","UNSC","GULL","CORM","BRCO","DCCO","PECO","HUMM","WEGU","BRPE")
RichnessCounts <- RawData[!RawData$Species%in%DropList,]

# Now select Spring survey data only, since only a few Fall surveys were conducted
RichnessCounts <- RichnessCounts[RichnessCounts$Season=="Spring",]

# Total number of detections per species per island and year
SpeciesCounts <- with(RichnessCounts,aggregate(Cluster_Size,by=list(Island,Year,Species),FUN=sum))
names(SpeciesCounts) <- c("Island","Year","Species","TotalCount")
```

```
###############################################################################################
#
# For each island, produce a plot showing which species were detected each year

# Open a .png graphics file for the island
png("AN_Richness.png", res=200, width=6, height=8, units="in") # make the graph 8 inches high by 6 in wide
    tempD <- SpeciesCounts[SpeciesCounts$Island=="AN", ]
    tempD <- merge(tempD,SPlist,by.x="Species",by.y="Species",all.x=TRUE)
    p=qplot(Common_Name, Year, data=tempD, xlab="Species",
        main="Species Detected on East Anacapa Island")+
        geom_point() + coord_flip()
    print(p)
dev.off()

# Open a .png graphics file for the island
png("SB_Richness.png", res=200, width=6, height=8, units="in") # make the graph 8 inches high by 6 in wide
```

```
    tempD <- SpeciesCounts[SpeciesCounts$Island=="SB",]
    tempD <- merge(tempD,SPlist,by.x="Species",by.y="Species",all.x=TRUE)
    p=qplot(Common_Name, Year, data=tempD, xlab="Species",
        main="Species Detected on Santa Barbara Island")+
        geom_point() + coord_flip()
    print(p)
dev.off()

# Open a .png graphics file for the island
png("SC_Richness.png", res=200, width=6, height=8, units="in") # make the graph 8 inches high by 6 in wide
    tempD <- SpeciesCounts[SpeciesCounts$Island=="SC",]
    tempD <- merge(tempD,SPlist,by.x="Species",by.y="Species",all.x=TRUE)
    p=qplot(Common_Name, Year, data=tempD, xlab="Species",
        main="Species Detected on Santa Cruz Island")+
        geom_point() + coord_flip()
    print(p)
dev.off()

# Open a .png graphics file for the island
png("SM_Richness.png", res=200, width=6, height=8, units="in") # make the graph 8 inches high by 6 in wide
    tempD <- SpeciesCounts[SpeciesCounts$Island=="SM",]
    tempD <- merge(tempD,SPlist,by.x="Species",by.y="Species",all.x=TRUE)
    p=qplot(Common_Name, Year, data=tempD, xlab="Species",
        main="Species Detected on San Miguel Island")+
        geom_point() + coord_flip()
    print(p)
dev.off()

# Open a .png graphics file for the island
png("SR_Richness.png", res=200, width=6, height=8, units="in") # make the graph 8 inches high by 6 in wide
    tempD <- SpeciesCounts[SpeciesCounts$Island=="SR",]
    tempD <- merge(tempD,SPlist,by.x="Species",by.y="Species",all.x=TRUE)
    p=qplot(Common_Name, Year, data=tempD, xlab="Species",
        main="Species Detected on Santa Rosa Island")+
        geom_point() + coord_flip()
    print(p)
dev.off()

##################################################################################
#
# Print out the table of Species Richness counts for each island and Year
SpeciesRich.table <- with(SpeciesCounts,table(Year,Island))
cat("Species Richness by Island and Year\n\n")
print(SpeciesRich.table,zero.print = "") # leave zeros as blanks because that Island and Year probably wasn't
sampled

# dataframe for plotting
SpeciesRich <- data.frame(with(SpeciesCounts,table(Year,Island)))
names(SpeciesRich)[3] <- "SpeciesRichness"
```

```
################################################################################
#
# Code for plotting out multi-panel graph with species richness by island for Spring counts
png("RichnessByIsland.png", res=200, width=8, height=6, units="in") # make the graph 6 inches high by 8
inches wide
  p=ggplot(aes(x=Year, y=SpeciesRichness), data=SpeciesRich) + geom_bar() + facet_grid(Island ~ .)
  print(p)
dev.off()
```

Table SOP 8-1. Example of table produced in Word by the R scripts above, to summarize species detected on point counts on Santa Barbara Island in Spring 2011. The total number of individuals of each species detected during 16 point counts is shown, along with the mean and standard error for the 16 stations counted, the number of stations on which the species was detected, and the percent of stations on which the species was detected.

Species	Common Name	#Detected	Mean	S.E.	# Stns	% Stns
AMKE	American Kestrel	2	0.12	0.09	2	12.5
GREG	Great Egret	1	0.06	0.06	1	6.2
HOLA	Horned Lark	89	5.56	0.84	15	93.8
OCWA	Orange-crowned Warbler	3	0.19	0.19	1	6.2
ROWR	Rock Wren	1	0.06	0.06	1	6.2
SAPH	Say's Phoebe	4	0.25	0.14	3	18.8
WCSP	White-crowned Sparrow	19	1.19	0.53	6	37.5
WEME	Western Meadowlark	54	3.38	0.55	14	87.5

Figure SOP 8-1. Example of a graphic produced by the R code above, showing number of species detected on both line transects and point counts on each of the islands between 1993 and 2011.

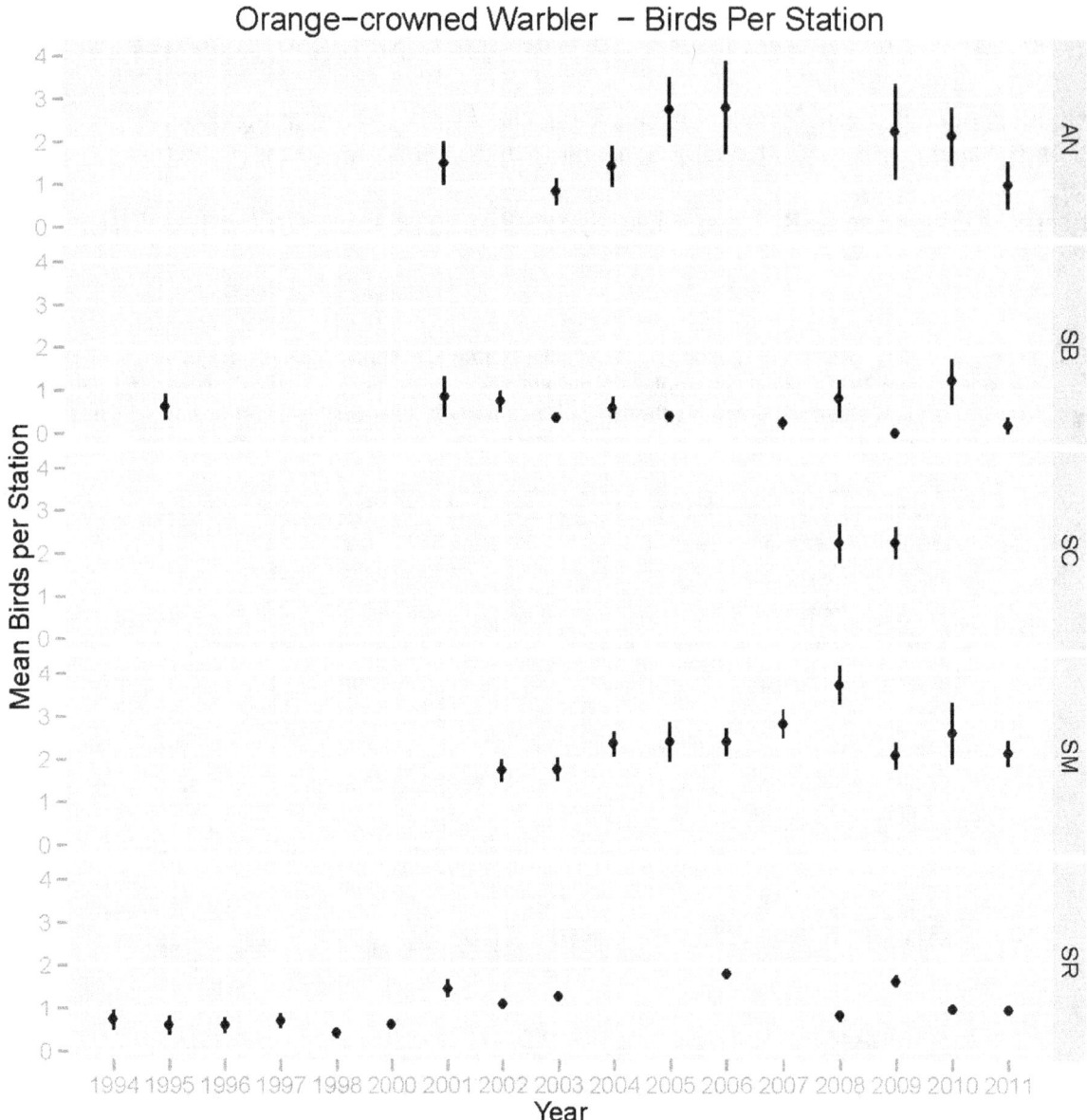

Figure SOP 8-2. Example of a graphic produced by the R code above, showing the mean birds per station and Standard Error for Orange-crowned Warbler on each island between 1993 and 2011.

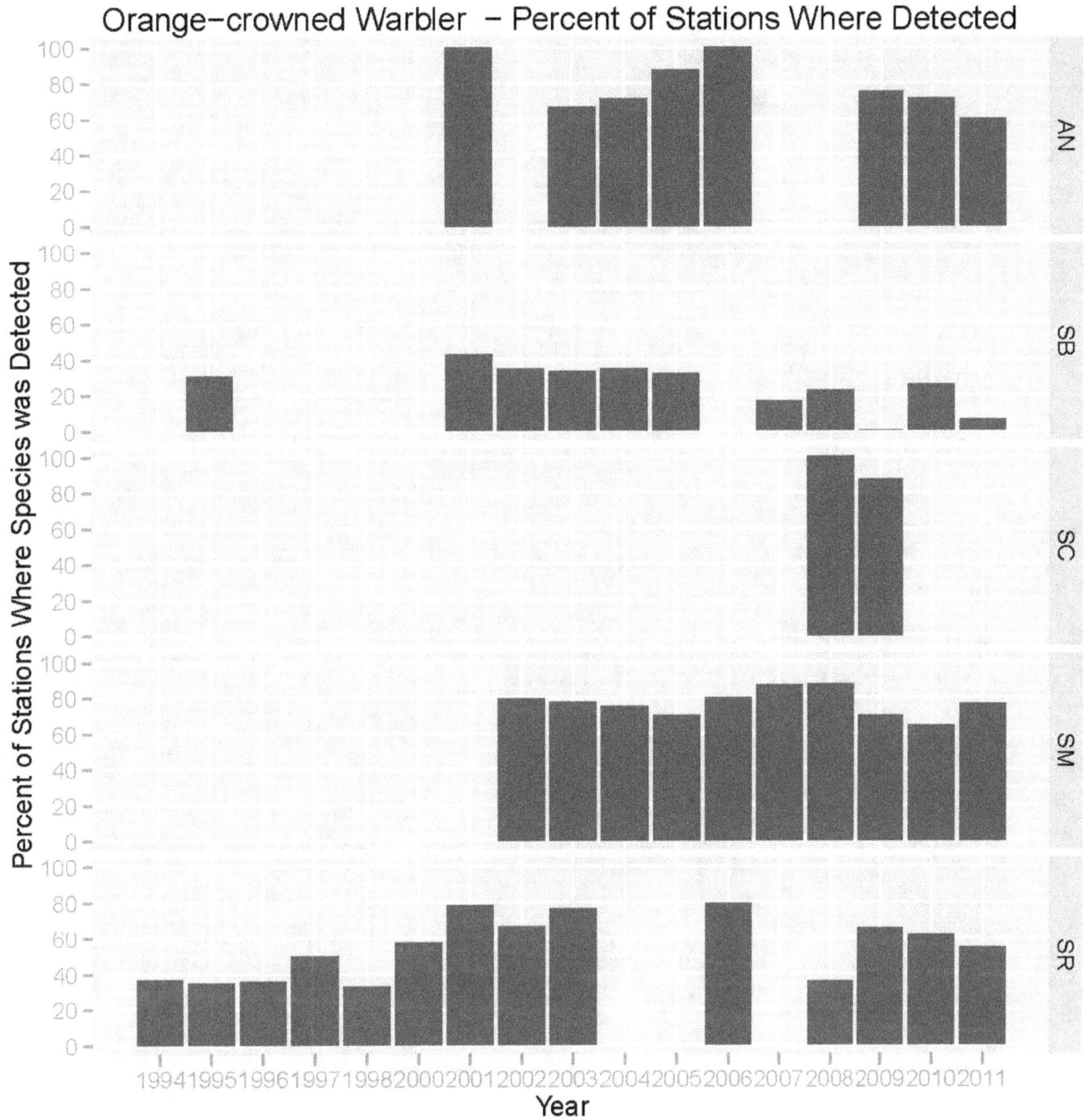

Figure SOP 8-3. Example of a graphic produced by the R code above, showing the percent of stations each island and each year on which Orange-crowned Warbler were detected during point counts.

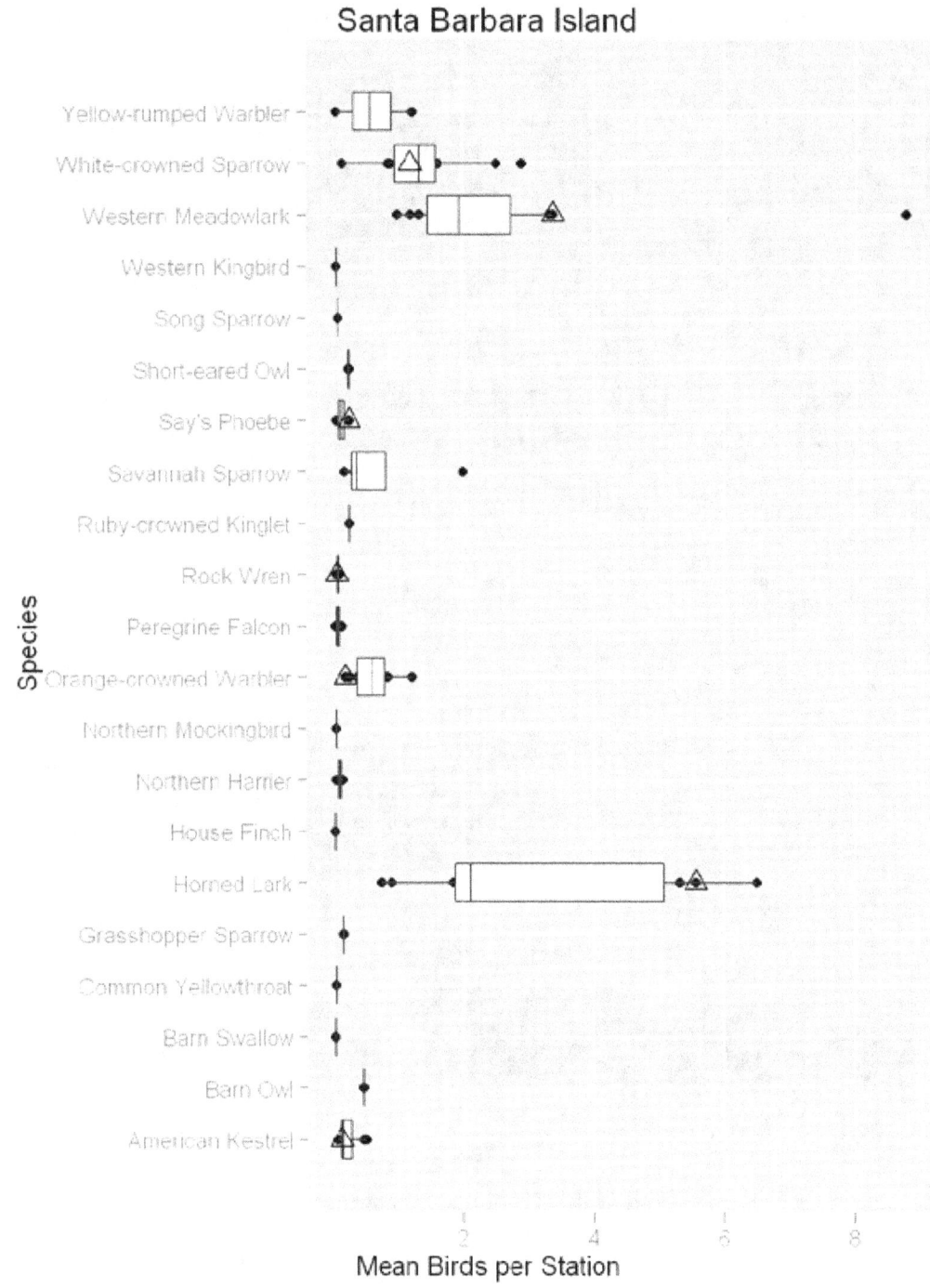

Figure SOP 8-4. Example of a graphic produced by the R code above, showing the mean birds per station for each species on Santa Barbara Island in 2011 (triangle around a point) in comparison to a boxplot of annual means for other years between 1993-2011.

Figure SOP 8-5. Example of a graphic produced by the R code above, showing the mean birds per station for each species on Santa Barbara Island in 2011 (triangle around a point) in comparison to a boxplot of annual means for other years between 1993-2011.

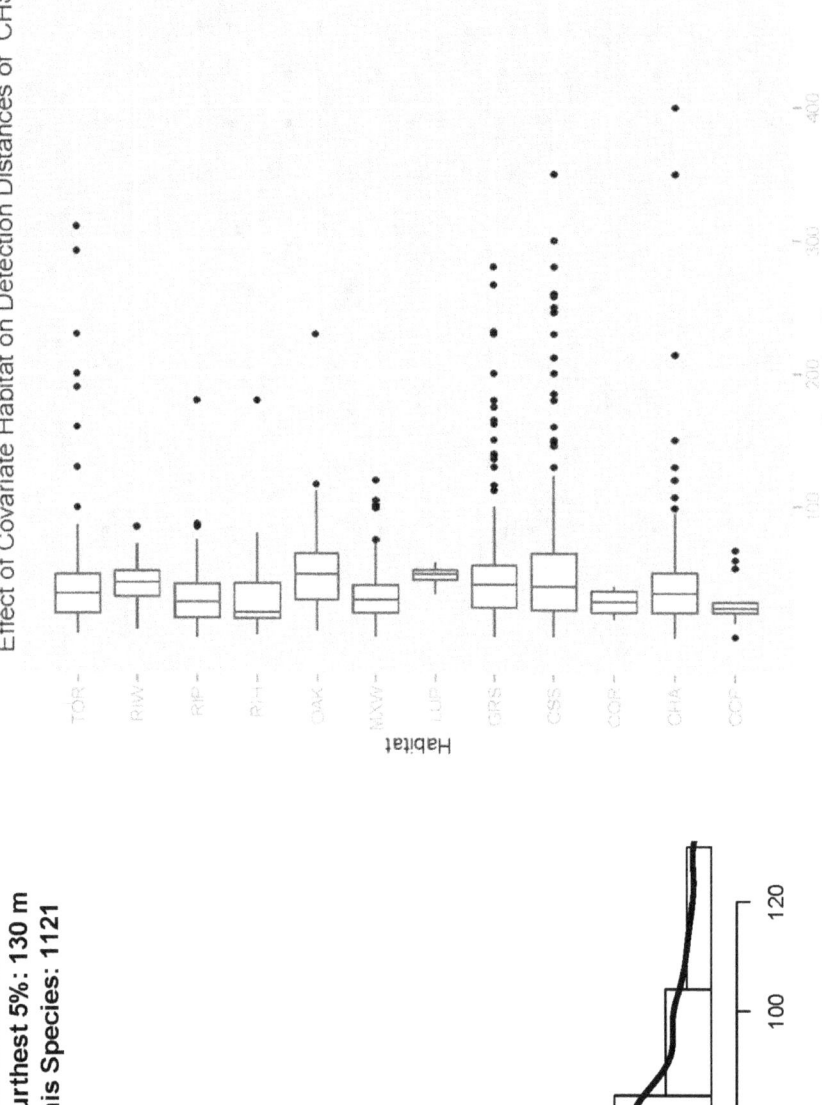

Effect of Covariate Habitat on Detection Distances of CHSP

Habitat

Detection Distance (m)

Figure SOP 8-7. Example of a graphic produced by the R code in CHIS_R_Scripts_DISTANCE.R to inspect the effect of the covariate Habitat type on detection distances of Song Sparrow between 1993-2011.

Distribution of Detection Distances for CHSP
Max. Distance after Truncating Furthest 5%: 130 m
Total Number of Distances for this Species: 1121

Density

Distance

Figure SOP 8-6. Example of a graphic produced by the R code in CHIS_R_Scripts_DISTANCE.R to inspect detection distances of Song Sparrow detected on point counts from all islands between 1993-2011.

Data Analysis using Program DISTANCE
Version 1.00 (2011)

Distance sampling is a robust, widely accepted method for estimating abundance of landbirds (Buckland et al. 2001, 2004) which makes it possible to estimate the probability of detecting a particular species (i.e., detection probability). Estimating the distance to each bird allows density to be approximated via a species-specific detection function that accounts for variation in detectability due to observer, habitat type, or weather-related factors. Based on the sampling design and sample sizes that we have developed for CHIS, we will be able to estimate density annually for a suite of common landbird species in the park, and by pooling data across multiple years, it will also be possible to calculate annual density estimates for some less-common species. There will be a number of rare or uncommon species for which we will not be able to obtain enough detections to develop a detection function – for these, we must use the raw, unadjusted counts of individuals seen or heard and the percent of plots on which the species was detected over time to evaluate status and trend.

Computing and Selecting Detectability Parameters

At least once every five years, we will conduct an analysis of factors influencing the detectability of birds and will develop detectability models to be used in estimating density of birds from raw counts. The NPS I&M Program provided some of the funding for the development of the free software program *Distance* (Thomas et al. 2005) and some of the statistical routines used in its analysis engines. This SOP provides some guidelines on use of Version 6 of the *Distance* software to model detectability and estimate density of landbirds at CHIS. The software, user guide, and training materials can be downloaded for free from http://www.ruwpa.st-and.ac.uk/distance/.

This Standard Operating Procedure (SOP) provides some guidelines for analyzing CHIS bird data in *Distance*, but explaining in detail how to use the software or providing a primer on analytical techniques associated with distance sampling is beyond its scope. The guidelines here are copied or modified from those in SOP 16 of the landbird monitoring protocol developed by the Sierra Nevada I&M Network (Siegel et al. 2010). *Distance* includes a user-friendly interface and a user's manual that explains how to use the software. The user's manual assumes that the user is already familiar with distance sampling concepts and statistics. Data analysts seeking help with the analytical aspects of distance sampling should consult Buckland et al. (2001) and, for a discussion of more advanced topics, Buckland et al. (2004).

Numerous factors may influence detectability, including species, habitat, observer, year, and perhaps other variables. Some of these factors are likely to vary over time or space, and therefore must be accounted for before: (1) density estimates can be made, and (2) trends in density can be assessed. Data analysis should identify and correct for any substantial sources of variation in detectability, to the extent sample sizes allow. For common species, the analyst will model detection probabilities based on species detections amassed during the multi-year analysis period. For rarer species, it may be necessary to derive detection models using more extensive data sets that contain all bird monitoring data collected at CHIS to date. By having all data at his or her disposal, the analyst retains flexibility to test effects of variables such as habitat, year, and observer on detection probability where sample sizes allow, and develop the best possible detectability functions for rarer species.

The CHIS *LB.mdb* database includes a data export routine to facilitate the importing of data into *Distance* for analysis. Detection functions must be developed for one species at a time, and separate detection functions are necessary for Point Counts versus Line Transects. This is because in the case of Point Counts, the area being surveyed increases with distance intervals from the observer, e.g., the area within the circular band between 10 and 20 m away from the observer is less than the area of the band between 20 and 30 m from the observer.

In the *LB.mdb* database under the Reporting tab, click on the Export to Distance button to create a text file that is formatted for import to *Distance*. Select either Point Counts or Line Transects, and then select a species, and click OK. The filename of the export file will contain the species code, count type (PC or LT), and the date and time of file creation. The first record in the export file is the header line that is correctly formatted for *Distance* to specify each of the columns of data and tells *Distance* where to store the data in its data structure. For example, the following lines show the header record for point count detections of House Finch (HOFI) at 10 point count stations on Santa Rosa Island in 1995. There were no detections of HOFI at stations LC01 through LC05 or at LC08, and two HOFI were detected at station LC09.

Study area*Label	Region*Label	Point transect*Label	Point transect*Survey effort	Observation*Radial distance	Observation*Flocksize	Observation*OBs	Observation*Species
CHIS	SR-1995	LC01	1				
CHIS	SR-1995	LC02	1				
CHIS	SR-1995	LC03	1				
CHIS	SR-1995	LC04	1				
CHIS	SR-1995	LC05	1				
CHIS	SR-1995	LC06	1	68	1	TJC	HOFI
CHIS	SR-1995	LC07	1	31	1	TJC	HOFI
CHIS	SR-1995	LC08	1				
CHIS	SR-1995	LC09	1	39	2	TJC	HOFI
CHIS	SR-1995	LC09	1	62	1	TJC	HOFI
CHIS	SR-1995	LC10	1	36	3	TJC	HOFI

Follow general instructions provided in the *Distance* User's Manual and the steps and screen captures below under "Importing Data into Distance" to create a project and import data. Although step-by-step instructions are beyond the scope of this SOP, suggestions below should help in successfully navigating through portions of the user interface that may be confusing.

- In the New Project Setup Wizard, at "Step 3: Survey Methods", choose "Point transect" as the Type of Survey.
- At Step 5, it is not necessary to select any multiplier options if the project will be used only for modeling detectability (that is, if it will not be used for calculating density estimates, which may be treated as a separate step from detectability estimation).

Once data have been successfully imported, use the Analysis tab to construct and test detectability models. Then use criteria including Akaike Information Criterion, model fit statistics, and biological 'reasonableness' of the models to determine whether a better model was fit by including habitat as a covariate. The same general approach may be used to assess other potential sources of variation in detectability, including observer and year. Other sources may be important as well; there is no substitute for thorough data exploration.

Alternately, the multiple covariates distance sampling (MCDS) engine in the *Distance* software may be used to model potential sources of variation in detectability as covariates of the scale parameter of the key function. Using this method, the covariates are assumed to influence the scale of the detection function, but not its shape; that is, the covariates affect the rate at which detectability decreases with distance, but not the overall shape of the detection curve.

Once the analyst is satisfied that the best possible models of detectability for each species have been developed, he or she should record the essential parameters of the selected model(s) for each species—truncation point (w), detection probability estimate (P), standard error of the detection probability estimate (*se* of P), and degrees of freedom of the detection probability estimate (*df* of P). All of these values should be reported in the report.

Estimating Density

Once the detectability model parameters have been derived, they should be used to estimate density of each species at each point, for all years under consideration. To estimate point-specific densities for a particular year in *Distance*, begin by querying the landbird monitoring database to create a text file containing all of the point count detections for the year of interest. At a minimum, the text file will need to contain fields indicating the observer, habitat type, site code, species (4-letter codes will be most convenient), and the estimated distance from the observer. If other variables such as observer or year have also been found to affect detectability, they need be included as well. A few things to keep in mind when creating the text file:

- Detections classified in the database as 'flyovers' should be omitted from the text file.
- There must be at least one record for every point that was surveyed in the year of interest. For points where no birds were detected, there should be a single record with species = 'None'. Failure to account for points with no detections will cause an upward bias in the results.
- Distance will not perform the calculations correctly if the records are not sorted properly. For the density estimations, the records must be sorted by point, such that all the records for each species at each point are grouped together in the database.

Import the text file into *Distance*. At Step 5 of the New Project Setup Wizard be sure to check the box indicating "Add Multipliers for: Other". When running the calculations for each species and each set of habitats, use the Data tab to enter the appropriate multiplier (detection probability) estimate, standard error, and degrees of freedom values from the modeling efforts in Section 2 above. Use the Data Filter to specify not only the species, but also the truncation point, which should be the distance used for generating the models (see section 2, above). Remember to change the multiplier and truncation values each time analysis is conducted on a new species.

When defining models, select the uniform key function with no series expansions—this way the program will simply use the parameter values you have specified, without constructing new models. Specifying Sample under "Level of Resolution of Estimates" in the Model Definition Properties box will instruct the program to return a density estimate of the species indicated in the Data Filter at each survey point.

Importing Data into Distance

The following screen captures illustrate the steps involved in creating a new Project in Distance and importing data from the CHIS_LB database to a Distance project. A separate Project will need to be created for each species, and separate projects must also be set up for Line Transects versus Point Counts because there are different analysis and modeling routines needed for these two types of surveys.

The following example shows how to import data from point counts to develop detection functions and calculate densities for House Finch (HOFI). The Distance software will create a new project folder called HOFI.dat and the data will be stored in a file DistData.mdb in the HOFI.dat folder.

The Export to Distance routine in the database creates a text file for HOFI point counts with the date and time when the file was created. This .txt file will be imported into a Distance Project that we will name HOFI-PC. To begin, run the Distance.exe program and select "Create a New Project".

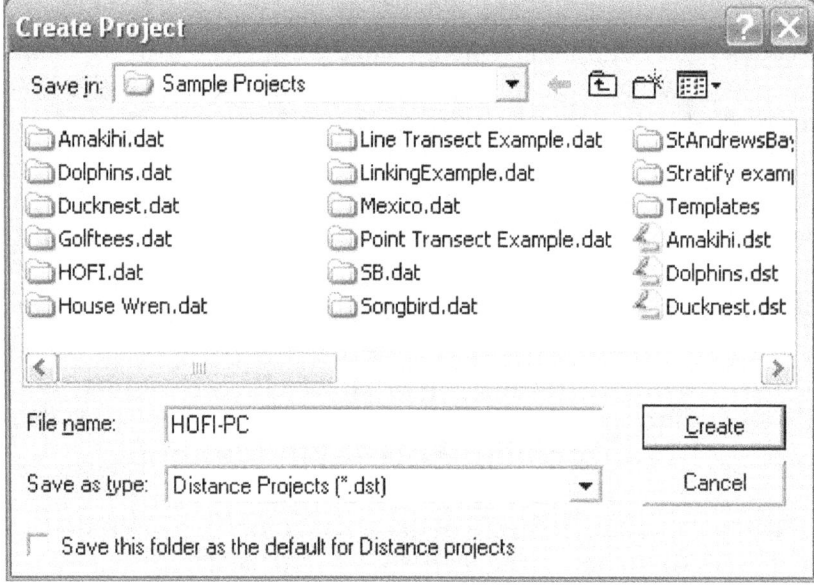

Next, after clicking on Create to get into the Project Setup wizard, select "Analyze a survey that has been completed":

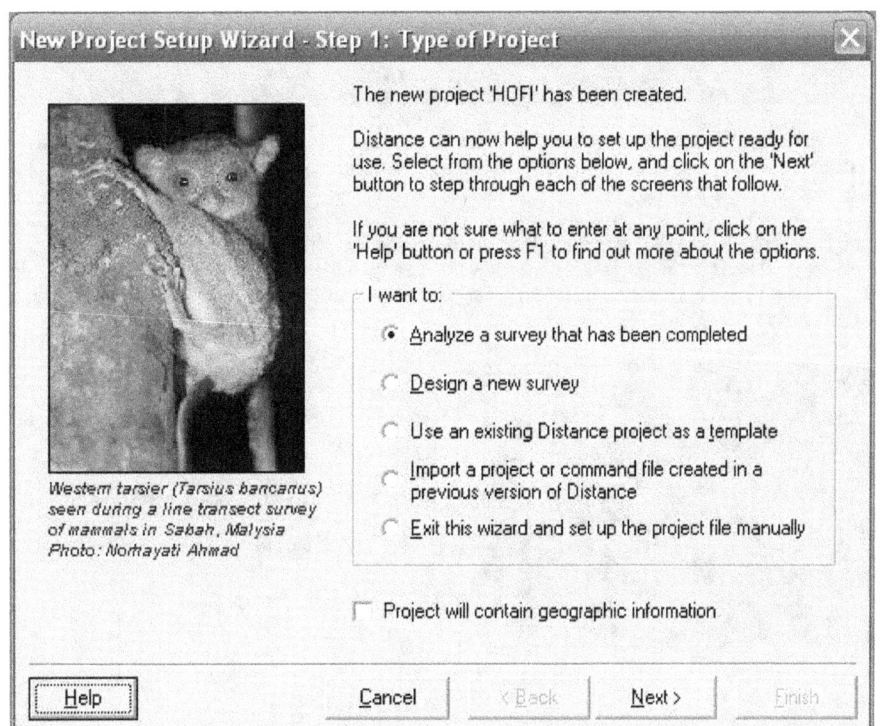

Western tarsier (Tarsius bancanus) seen during a line transect survey of mammals in Sabah, Malysia
Photo: Norhayati Ahmad

In the Survey Methods window, select Point Transect for the Type of Survey, and "Clusters of objects" for Observations:

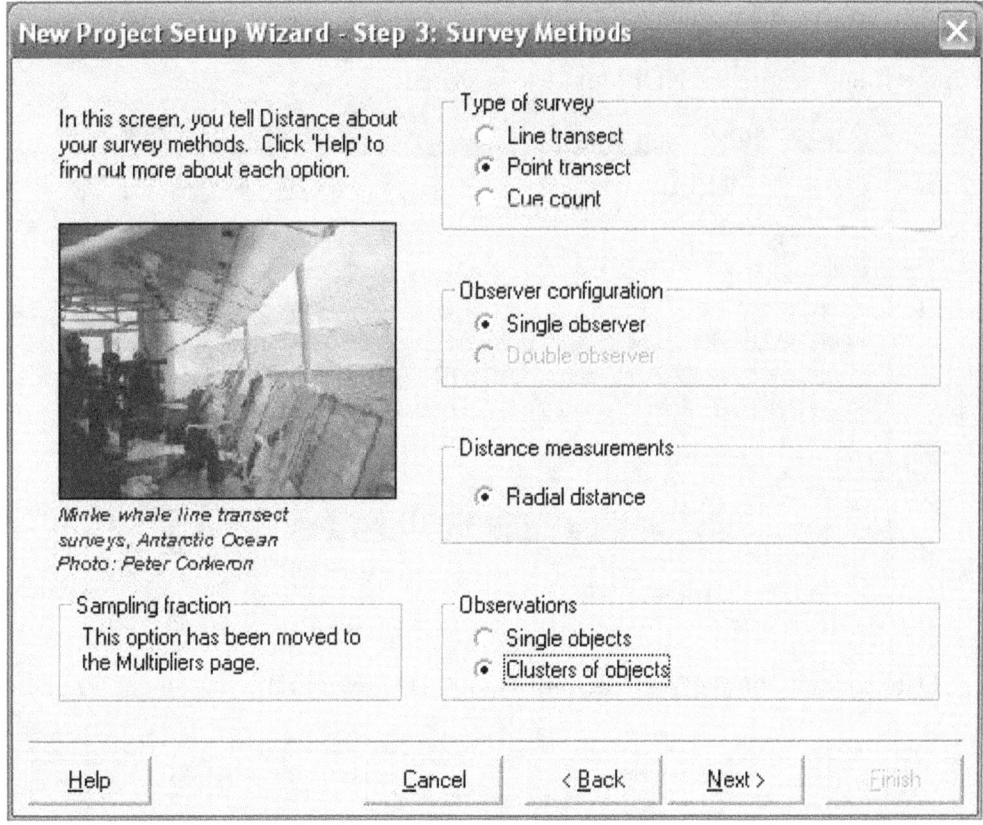

Minke whale line transect surveys, Antarctic Ocean
Photo: Peter Corkeron

Proceed to the Data Import Wizard:

Navigate to the folder where the HOFI text file is stored:

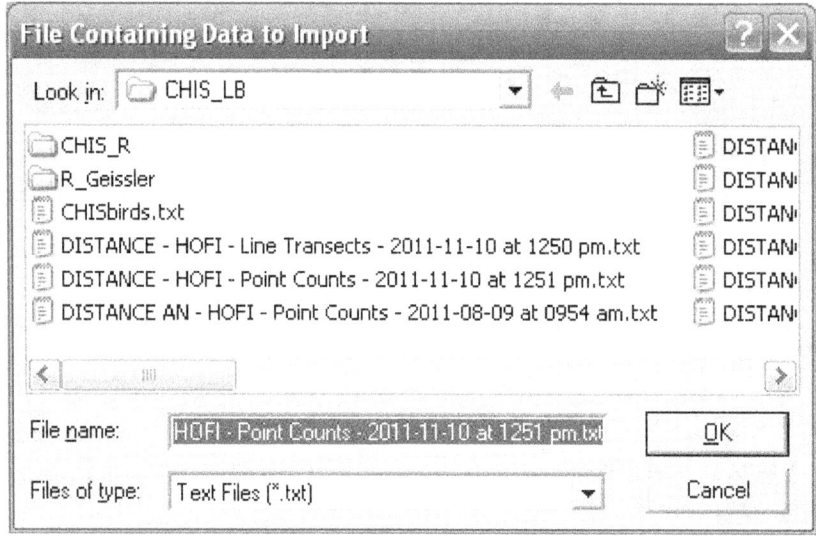

For Step 3: Data Destination, keep the default values as shown in the screen capture below:

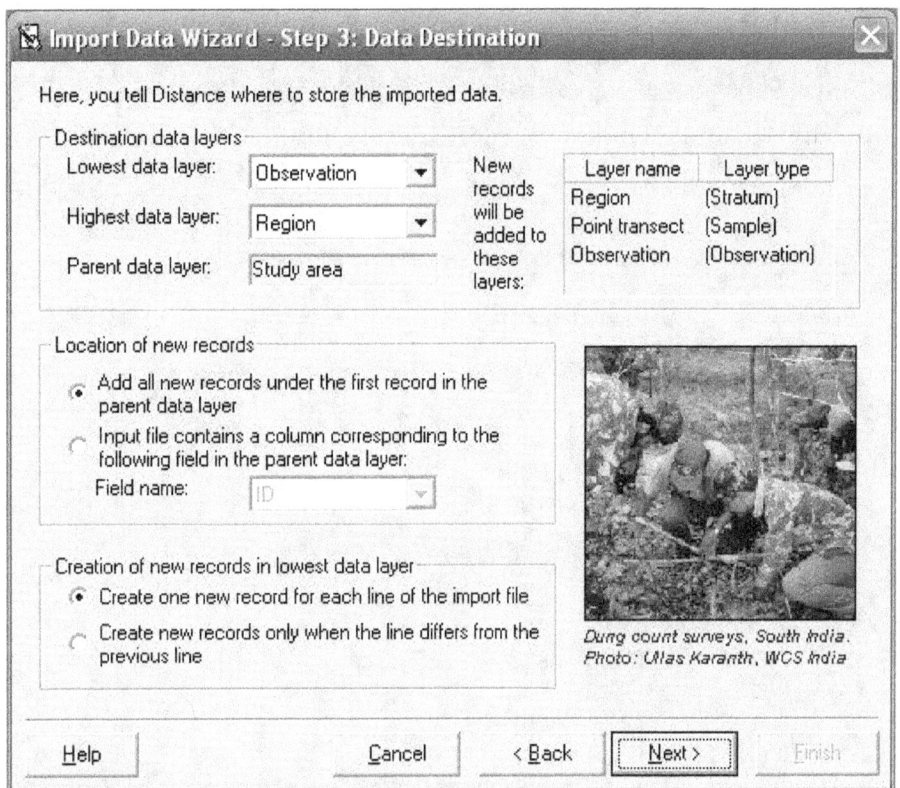

Dung count surveys, South India.
Photo: Ulas Karanth, WCS India

The HOFI text file is already formatted for Distance with tab delimiters, and the data should automatically import into the correct layers and columns in DistData.mdb as shown below:

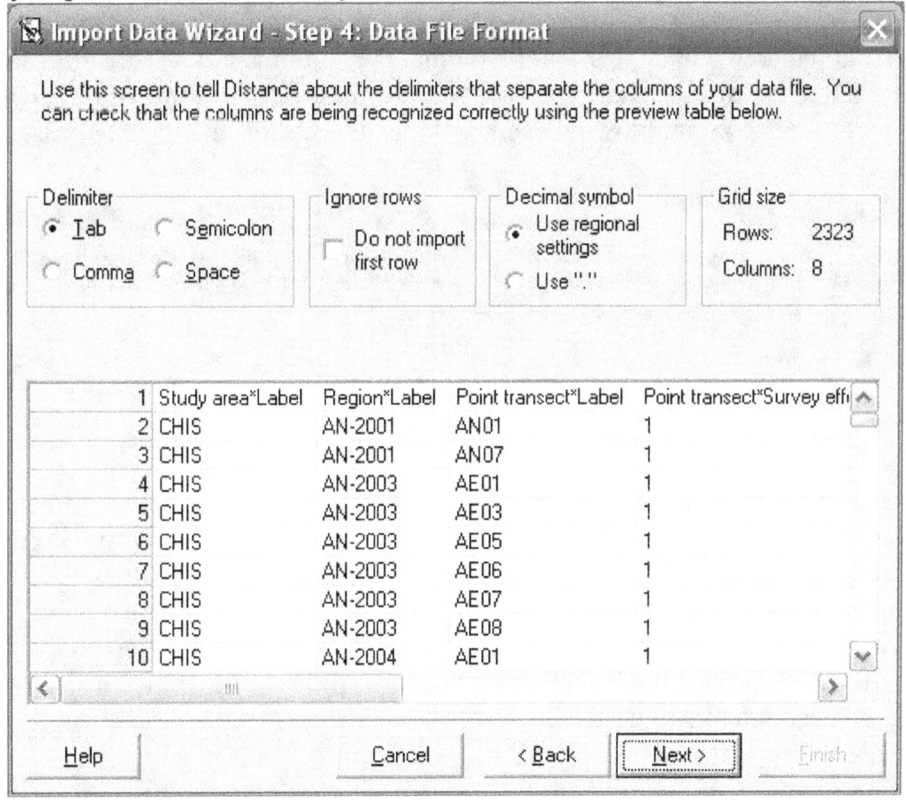

In Step 5, select "First row contains layer names and field names of each column":

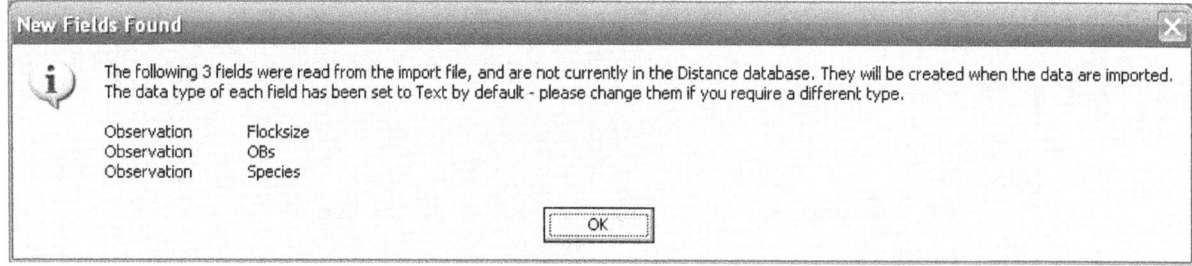

An informational window will appear to tell you that the columns Flocksize, OBs, and Species will also be added to the distance data file. We will use these data in some of our analyses, but they are not part of the default fields in Distance which is why this message appears:

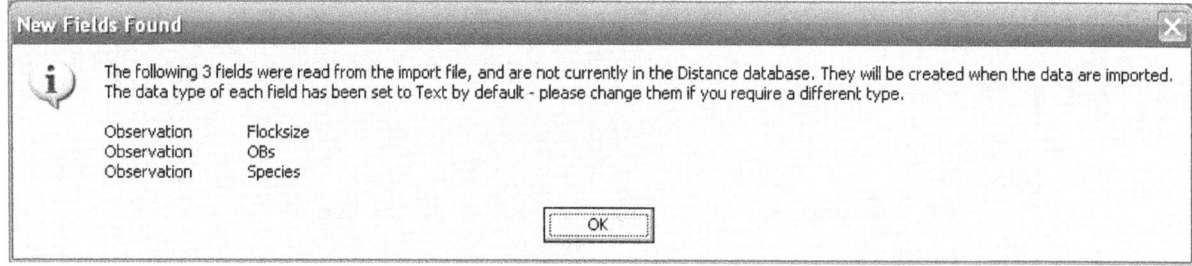

Our detection data for HOFI have now been imported into a Distance project, and are ready for analysis in Distance. The data have been imported into the Study Area, Region, Point Transect, and Observations layers as shown in the following two screen captures of how the data appear in the DistData.mdb file created by Distance. In our case, the Region will be a combination of the Island and Year, which will allow us to pool all distances in order to develop an overall detection function for each bird species, but it will also allow us to produce separate density estimates for each Island and Year combination.

An example of how the HOFI data appear in the Distance data browser is shown below. If a station was sampled during a particular survey but no House Finch were detected during that 10-minute count, the station will be included so that the sampling effort is included correctly, but the right-most five columns (e.g., Radial distance, OBs=Observer) will be blank as shown for some records below:

Distance - HOFI - [Project Browser]
File · Edit · View · Tools · Data · Window · Help

Data | Maps | Designs | Surveys | Analyses | Simulations

Data layers: Study area — Region — Point transect — Observation

Contents of Observation layer 'Observation' and all fields from higher layers

Study area		Region			Point transect			Observation					
ID	Label	ID	Label	Area	ID	Label	Survey effort	ID	Radial distance	Cluster size	Flocksize	OBs	Species
n/a	n/a	n/a	n/a	ha	n/a	n/a	[None]	n/a	m	[None]	n/a	n/a	n/a
Int	Int	Int	Int	Decimal	Int	Int	Int	Int	Decimal	Decimal	Text	Text	Text
1	HOFI	1	AN-2001	0	1	AN01	1						
					2	AN07	1						
					3	AE01	1						
					4	AE03	1						
		2	AN-2003	0	5	AE05	1						
					6	AE06	1						
					7	AE07	1						
					8	AE08	1						
					9	AE01	1						
					10	AE02	1						
					11	AE03	1						
		3	AN-2004	0	12	AE05	1	1	50	1	15	LCD	HOFI
					13	AE06	1						
					14	AE07	1						
					15	AE08	1						
					16	AE01	1						
					17	AE02	1						
					18	AE03	1						
		4	AN-2005	0	19	AE04	1						
					20	AE05	1						
					21	AE06	1						
					22	AE07	1						
					23	AE08	1						
					24	AE03	1						
		5	AN-200E	0	25	AE05	1	2	9	1	2	CEV	HOFI
								3	9	1	2	CEV	HOFI
								4	13	1	1	CEV	HOFI
					26	AE06	1	5	35	1	2	CEV	HOFI
								6	16	1	1	CEV	HOFI
					27	AE07	1						

Another view of the data as they appear in the Distance layers and data fields, for a 1994 survey on Santa Rosa Island:

Distance - HOFI - [Project Browser]

File   Edit   View   Tools   Data   Window   Help

Data

Maps   Designs   Surveys   Analyses   Simulations

Data layers
- Study area
  - Region
    - Point transect
      - Observation

Contents of Observation layer 'Observation' and all fields from higher layers

Study area		Region			Point transect			Observation					
ID	Label	ID	Label	Area	ID	Label	Survey effort	ID	Radial distance	Cluster size	Flocksize	OBs	Species
				ha					m				
n/a	n/a	n/a	n/a	Decimal	n/a	n/a	Decimal	n/a	Decimal	Decimal	n/a	n/a	n/a
Int	Int	Int	Int	Int	Int	Int	Int	Int	Int	Int	Int	Int	Int
					702	LC03	1	128	24	1	1	TJC	HOFI
					703	LC04	1						
					704	LC05	1						
					705	LC06	1						
					706	LC07	1	129	12	1	1	TJC	HOFI
								130	15	1	1	TJC	HOFI
								131	5	1	1	TJC	HOFI
					707	LC08	1						
					708	LC09	1						
					709	LC10	1	132	30	1	1	TJC	HOFI
					710	LC11	1	133	48	1	8	TJC	HOFI
					711	LC12	1	134	45	1	1	TJC	HOFI
					712	LC13	1	135	14	1	1	TJC	HOFI
					713	LC14	1						
1	HOFI	32	SR-1994	0	714	LC15	1						
					715	LC16	1						
					716	LC17	1						
					717	LC18	1	136	30	1	1	TJC	HOFI
					718	LC19	1						
					719	LC20	1						
					720	TP01	1	137	9	1	1	TJC	HOFI
					721	TP02	1						
					722	TP03	1						
					723	TP04	1	138	7	2	2	TJC	HOFI
					724	TP05	1						
					725	TP06	1	139	21	1	1	TJC	HOFI
					726	TP07	1	140	41	1	1	TJC	HOFI
					727	TP08	1	141	32	1	1	TJC	HOFI
					728	TP09	1	142	18	2	2	TJC	HOFI
								143	35	1	1	TJC	HOFI

Channel Islands National Park Landbird Monitoring Protocol

Standard Operating Procedure (SOP) # 10

After the Field Season
Version 1.00 (2011)

Revision History Log:

Prev. Version #	Revision Date	Author	Changes Made	Reason for Change	New Version #

This Standard Operating Procedure (SOP) provides a brief summary of post-season procedures for landbird monitoring in Channel Islands National Park. Observers should be familiar with and follow these procedures after the field season is completed.

Procedures:

1. Equipment must be cleaned, repaired, and returned to the proper storage areas in the park RM Annex. All references manuals, materials, and extra data sheets should be returned to the Landbird Program Manager to be filed or re-shelved in their appropriate storage location in the RM Annex.

2. Field data sheets should be organized and checked to be sure that they have been filled out completely. Checking for completeness should generally be done before leaving the field. Original datasheets are scanned to pdf for each field event (tour) and then given to the Landbird Program Manager for eventual archive with Cultural Resource staff. The Landbird Program Manager will keep a copy in the RM Annex Office for reference. Data may be entered in the field using the macro upload database, or in the office on the main server.

3. All landbird monitoring datasheets, reference manuals, and equipment are stored with the Landbird Program Manager:

>Landbird Program Manager
>Channel Islands National Park
>1431 Spinnaker Drive
>Ventura CA 93003

Channel Islands National Park Landbird Monitoring Protocol

Standard Operating Procedure (SOP) # 11

Revising the Protocol Narrative and SOPs
Version 1.00 (2011)

Revision History Log:

Prev. Version #	Revision Date	Author	Changes Made	Reason for Change	New Version #

This Standard Operating Procedure (SOP) explains how to make and track changes to the Landbird Protocol Narrative and associated SOPs for Channel Islands National Park. Over time, the protocol narrative and SOPs may require modifications. The following procedures must be followed when making changes to ensure that previous data collection and processing procedures are clearly understood when using and interpreting historical data sets. Similarly, clearly articulating new methods is key to credible interpretation of data acquired since the implementation of changes. Personnel making changes must be familiar with this SOP to ensure that proper reviews are conducted, and that documentation standards are followed.

Procedures:

1. Modifications must be reviewed for clarity and technical soundness. Small changes or additions to existing methods will be reviewed in-house by Inventory and Monitoring management staff. An outside review will be done for whole-scale changes in methods. Regional and national staff of the National Park Service and experts outside of the NPS with familiarity in bird monitoring and data analysis should be asked to review major changes.

2. All changes must be documented, and updated protocol versions must be recorded in the Revision History Log that accompanies the Protocol Narrative and each SOP. Changes are recorded only in the Protocol Narrative or the SOP being modified. Version numbers increase incrementally by hundredths (e.g. version 1.01, version 1.02, etc.) for minor changes. Major revisions will be designated with the next whole number (e.g., version 2.0, 3.0, 4.0 ...). Record the previous version number, date of revision, author of the revision, identify the paragraphs and pages where changes were made, and record the reason for the changes along with the new version number.

3. Narrative and SOP updates may occur independently. That is, a change in one SOP will not necessarily invoke changes in other SOPs, and a narrative update may not require SOP modifications. All narrative and SOP version changes must be noted in the Master Version Table (MVT), which is maintained in this SOP. Any time a narrative or an SOP version change occurs, a new Version Key number (VK#) must be created and recorded in the MVT,

along with the date of the change and the versions of the narrative and SOPs in effect. The VK number increments by whole integers (e.g., 1, 2, 3, 4, 5). Updates to the MVT will be documented by the Landbird Program Manager for inclusion in the master version table database. The Version Key number is essential for project information to be properly interpreted and analyzed. The protocol narrative, SOPs, and data should not be distributed independently of this table.

4. New versions of the Protocol Narrative and SOPs must be posted on the network web page and uploaded to the NPS Vital Signs and Protocol Database. Previous versions of the Protocol Narrative and SOPs must be archived in the Protocol Library for the Mediterranean Coast I&M Network.

Landbird Monitoring Protocol for Channel Islands National Park

Table SOP 11-1. Master Version Table

Version Key #	Date of Change	Narrative	SOP #1	SOP #2	SOP #3	SOP #4	SOP #5	SOP #6	SOP #7	SOP #8	SOP #9	SOP #10
VK1	XX-X-20XX	1.00	1.00	1.00	1.00	1.00	1.00	1.00	1.00	1.00	1.00	1.0

NPS 159/112106, December 2011